THE FOREVER YOUNGS

The Three Kinds of People we Meet

KYLE JAY BECKWERMERT

Copyright © 2017 KYLE JAY BECKWERMERT

All rights reserved.

DEDICATION

To Mom and Dad:

for teaching me how to love rather than to hate,
and to lead rather than to follow.

CONTENTS

INTRODUCTION 1

THE THREE KINDS OF PEOPLE 3

LEAVE THE TRIBE BEHIND 15

BE PLAYFUL 27

LET GO OF YOUR BODY 37

QUIT WORRYING 61

TRUST THE TIMING OF YOUR LIFE 73

RULE YOUR THOUGHTS, RULE YOUR WORLD 85

HAPPY FOOD, HAPPY YOU 99

PUSH THROUGH FAILURE 115

FINAL THOUGHTS 121

THE AFFIRMATIONS 125

INTRODUCTION

The purpose of this book is to help you reconnect with your essence. Your essence is timeless, boundless, and infinite. It has no form, it knows no limits. It is the core of who you are as a human being. When you connect with this essence, marvellous events transpire. You will feel peace and joy, no matter what turbulence surrounds you, and your body will transform in ways that will literally allow you to defy time. Those who have found this connection are known as "the Forever Youngs." And these people think and see the world differently than most. The intent of this book is to help you think, feel, and act as they do. They have discovered their greatness, and so to will you once you correct the way you think.

What separates a human being from this essence is simply this thought: "I am not good enough." All our suffering originates from this belief. It is the source of all disease and unhappiness in this world. When we learn to love ourselves, when we believe we are good enough, we connect with our essence, and all our troubles cease to exist.

It is my hope that you rediscover that eternal part of you, for when you do, you will inherent a vitality that can never be shaken—a vitality that has the capacity to heal your life, manifest your desires, and above all else, allow you to remain Forever Young in body, mind, and spirit.

1

THE THREE KINDS OF PEOPLE

"One individual who lives and vibrates to the energy of pure love and reverence for all of life will counter-balance the negativity of 750,000 individuals who calibrate at the lower weakening levels."

-David Hawkins

Those who vibrate with the energy of love and reverence in this world are known as "the Forever Youngs." The Forever Youngs have connected with their essence and they have discovered their happiness, their excitement, and their purpose. Whenever you experience the feeling of happiness, you are tuning into your natural state of being. Finding this can be difficult; every day we're faced with conflict and struggles. But to master anything, we need to put in the time. It takes a sustained effort to see results. Happiness is your birthright, your obligation, and your purpose in this life and if we wish to become more fully functioning human beings, we must learn how to tune into this higher vibration. We raise this energy by changing the way we think and see the world. With that, there is a spectrum of energetic beings who vibrate at different levels of consciousness.

There are three kinds of people in this world: those who give energy, those who take energy, and those who do neither. The people who give energy are filled with positive thoughts. The people who take energy are filled with negative thoughts. And the people who neither take nor give energy are filled with complacent thoughts. Every person on the planet falls into one of these categories. We either empower others, disempower others, or have no effect on others. This book is meant to help you become the kind of person who gives energy. These are the people who walk this earth with happiness in their hearts and who have the profound ability to attract what they desire. They are the leaders, the creators, the peacekeepers, and the innovators of the world. They are the Forever Youngs.

The Forever Youngs vibrate with energy that can uplift and inspire the world around them. When you are around these special beings, you cannot help but feel calm and peaceful, for you pick up on their energy. It stems from the way they think and how they see the world. "We convince by our presence," said Walt Whitman. And when we vibrate at higher levels of consciousness through thoughts of bliss, we unconsciously influence other people's vibration as well. It is therefore wise to fill our minds with high-calibre thoughts (love, hope, and purpose) and surround ourselves with people who think likewise. Let's begin our journey of reconnecting with our essence by taking a closer look at the three types of people.

The Takers

At the bottom of the energetic totem pole are the people who take or absorb energy from the world. They are known as "the Takers," and it's incredibly easy to think and act as they do. The Takers complain, whine, sniffle, blame, and find fault. You can hear these individuals at the mall, in restaurants, at the gym, etc. They bicker about the weather or the traffic, and they often feel as if they're in the wrong place at the wrong time. We all know someone like this, don't we? We've all heard Takers say things such as, "Why is it raining today?" or "Well, Susy and her family have that, so why don't we?" The Takers feel victimized by life. They think every person is better off than they are, so they will always find a reason to grumble, despite how great things might be going in their lives. It doesn't matter if the service was flawless, the food was delicious, or the movie was riveting—they tend to spin positive into negative. The Takers create more problems than solutions. These individuals are so disconnected from their essence, you'll rarely see smiles on their faces, at least not authentic ones. They see the glass as half empty instead of half full.

The Takers generally feel inadequate and insecure based on that one simple thought: "I'm not good enough." It defines them. Consequently, they feel the need to seek approval and recognition from "the tribe," i.e., society, the crowd, others, the masses. The Takers' feelings are controlled by what the tribe thinks of them, not by what they think of themselves. Often, in order to feel worthy and valuable, they become obsessed with accumulating as much material wealth as possible, even at the expense of their own health. Their self-worth is based on what they have and what people think of them. Is it any wonder they're so pessimistic and frustrated all the time? There will always be someone with more things, and there will always be someone who doesn't like them—thus, there will always be a problem. The Takers see the world through a lens tainted with negativity.

Take great caution around these people. Their negativity and pessimistic view of the world can lower your own energy. You'll know when you're around them. A sense of anxiety, fear, or sluggishness will rise up within you. Not a word needs to be uttered by the Takers, as we can pick up on their energies when we're near them. You will experience their thoughts and perceptions of the world in every fibre of your being. Your body is a fine-tuned barometer of the energies around you. Listen to it. Trust your gut! As much as possible, steer clear of the energy suckers in your life, as they can cause much harm. Do your very best to surround yourself with high-calibre thoughts and people, for they will empower and bring out the best in you.

And before you say "Ugh, I know so many people like this—they make me so mad!" remember that these individuals are the ones experiencing the most hurt. They are the ones who feel abandoned, who feel they aren't good enough, and who feel a lack of love for themselves. Perhaps the next time you come across this kind of person, instead of getting frustrated and upset with them, give them silent words of encouragement: "May you find joy in your life, may you find peace in your life, and may you rediscover your self-importance."

The Floaters

Next on the energetic totem pole are those who simply accept the world as it is. They live their lives according to the tribe, and all the rules and regulations it imposes: be a good citizen, file your taxes, get a mortgage, go to college, get a job, save money, have kids, and, ultimately, retire. While this is all great and dandy, the Floaters lack two major things: excitement and purpose. They're mostly on autopilot, simply going through the motions of life to merely survive. They accept the cards that the world has dealt them. As time progresses, the Floaters become bored and complacent only to realize that life has passed them by and they have yet to find their happiness or purpose. The Floaters stay within their comfort zones and don't take the time to consult themselves and reflect on their desires. They might spend their whole lives in one job position, or vacationing at one spot, or ordering the same kind of food over and over again. They don't pursue greater opportunities for themselves because that involves risk, and they are risk averse. Playing it safe and staying within society's "guidelines" are common patterns among this group.

The root cause of the Floaters' behaviour can be easily overlooked. They may come across as well-functioning people, and to some degree they are, but they're doing things for the wrong reasons. They are fuelled by fear and by other people's opinions. They may be successful at their jobs, but these jobs don't excite or fulfill them. They build their lives around what the tribe has in mind for them and thus will never be fulfilled—their goals and dreams were never their own.

Like the Takers, the Floaters can be spotted in everyday conversations. They tend to need reassurance through praise and recognition, and can often be heard proclaiming how great they are. They boast about how well they have done for themselves in regards to their career, their parenting, etc. The Floaters can be self-centred, egotistical, and self-righteous, but at the end of the day, they feel a deep sense of emptiness within. This emptiness stems from living a life that is dull, safe, and comfortable. They see their life as good but not great, as fun but not electrifying, as ordinary but not extraordinary.

The Forever Youngs

And then there are the fully functioning individuals who reside at the highest level of consciousness on the energetic totem pole. Things that bother and irritate the average human being have little bearing on them. These individuals are often in a state of gratitude, and "worry" doesn't seem to be a part of their vocabulary. We've all been around these types of people, too. They are the people you meet and immediately connect with. For one reason or another, you feel the urge to talk to them on a deeper level, and it feels good to simply be in their presence. There is a gravitational pull that you can't explain, a magnetism. These people are filled with thoughts of love, hope, and harmony, and they exude serenity. There is little judgment, anxiety, or hatred in their hearts; in their world there is peace and purpose. These are the givers, the entrepreneurs, the visionaries, the go-getters, the leaders, and the creators, and their connection to essence is strong.

They are focused, growth orientated, and optimistic. Thus, they tend to be the most happy people.

You'll notice that these people disappear when negative dialogue occurs around them. It's almost as if they vanish by magic when drama unfolds — they have no time for self-defeating conversations, negative news, or people who promote anything other than peace and love. What governs the Forever Youngs' world is what they feel within, not what the tribe has in mind for them. It could be pouring rain, they could be stuck in traffic, or their plane could be delayed, yet they remain calm, unbothered, and content, for in their world everything is perfect. The Forever Youngs don't dwell on what's missing in their lives; rather, they put all their effort and awareness into what they do have. They do this because they understand that what you put your awareness on expands, and if we choose to focus on what's missing in our lives, we will continue to attract what's missing in our lives. So instead, they focus on gratitude, for the more we are thankful for, the more positive things will come our way.

Unlike the Floaters and the Takers, who lack direction and purpose, the Forever Youngs have a sense of their own destiny, an awareness of their mission in life. They understand that their time here on this earth is limited and that there are only so many days, so many heartbeats, to accomplish what it is they came here for. They see this limited time as a miracle and a blessing. They have a deep appreciation for the gift of life. For them, to experience all the senses and the riches of the world is a privilege. Breathing fresh air, possessing good health, walking down the sidewalk and feeling the sun shining on their face, laughing, dancing, playing, and singing, forming relationships and making lasting memories—all of these things are precious to them. As Walt Whitman so eloquently said, "Every cubic inch of space is a miracle." Most individuals don't think twice about life's seemingly ordinary experiences, and disregard them as routine events. However, the Forever Youngs experience excitement in these seemingly ordinary moments, which is what makes their perspective on the world so different from most. As you work on connecting with your essence and raising your consciousness, you'll find yourself naturally starting to see the world as extraordinary rather than ordinary.

Above all else, the Forever Youngs spend their lives in passion and on purpose—they have found their excitement. Everything else is just smoke, mirrors, and distractions. All the awards, all the certificates, all the degrees, and all the toys and riches in the world come secondary to a life of purpose. Furthermore, they have no interest in a life of neutrality. They want to make an impact and leave a legacy. The Forever Youngs are the people willing to take the risks, consult within, and go through the growing pains to find their greatness. They are not people pleasers or approval seekers, and thus they have no concern for what the tribe says or does. They are independent, open to change, and have a sense of self-worth based on who they are and not what they have. This is what we must strive for. In the following chapters, you'll begin to understand how these individuals conduct themselves in the world. And as a result, you will start seeing settle changes in your life as well. Worries and stresses that once took up so much of your attention will fade away and you'll discover yourself to be a far more powerful, courageous and purposeful human being.

Affirmation

I choose to surround myself with people who bring out the best in me, not people who bring out the stress in me. I will work on correcting my thoughts so that I may experience a higher level of awareness in my life. This higher level of awareness will allow me to create and lead the life I have envisioned for myself.

I am Forever Young

2

LEAVE THE TRIBE BEHIND

"Be who you are and say what you feel, because those who mind don't matter and those who matter don't mind."

-Theodor Seuss Geisel (Dr. Seuss)

Choosing to not care about what anyone else thinks of you is one of the most profound decisions you can make. There will always be someone who doesn't agree with you. No matter how hard you try, no matter how well you behave, no matter how smart you are or how funny and witty you are, there will always be someone who criticizes. Attempting to please everyone is a waste of time, energy, and effort. Instead, the Forever

Youngs are more concerned with how they see themselves, rather than how the world perceives them. Those who have made any impact in any profession have done so by not conforming to the tribe. By following our own calling, and disregarding what society thinks we should and shouldn't do, we will experience more personal freedom and peace in our lives.

You can't please everyone

If you're searching tirelessly for external validation, consider this: There are 8 billion people on this planet. Hypothetically speaking, 8 billion individuals will have their own perceptions of you and your behaviour. Can you imagine trying to make all of these people see the world the way you do? It would be a never-ending pursuit that would never fill your cup. Only you can do that. Unfortunately, so many people live their lives based on what others tell them. We as humans tend to act in accordance with what others (the tribe) say is right. We tend to follow the crowd instead of forging ahead on our own paths and building our own dreams. Most of the world is comfortable following, for leading requires strength, courage, and an ability to feel comfortable with uncertainty.

My question to you is this: why on earth would you concern yourself with someone else's reality, with someone else's ideas on how you should live your life? Others' beliefs and opinions have nothing to do with your karmic mission. Your karmic mission is simply your soul's purpose in this life. And each one of us has a different and unique assignment. Whether you're an actor, a firefighter, a business executive, or a salesman, when your soul's purpose is being fulfilled, you will feel peace, happiness, and joy.

I'm not saying you should drown out everyone who offers you advice or guidance; I'm saying listen to those who advocate your purpose and your passion and ignore everything else. True freedom and purpose never come from external validation. You must listen to your inner voice and ignore the crowd.

This life that you have chosen is uniquely yours. You are not here to fulfill someone else's karmic mission, and listening to anything but the voice in your head will surely result in end-of-life regret. As Steve Jobs said in his Stanford University commencement speech, "Your time is limited, so don't waste it living someone else's life. Don't be trapped by dogma—which is living with the results of other people's thinking. Don't let the noise of others' opinions drown out your own inner voice. And most important, have the courage to follow your heart and intuition."[1]

Perhaps you're thinking, "I don't know what my inner voice is saying," or, "I don't know what my mission is." Well, your mission is to do those things that make you smile, that motivate you to get up in the morning, that excite you on some idle Tuesday. That's it. That's all. Nothing more to it. Some of us were meant to be astronauts and some of us were meant to sell clothes. Some of us were meant to travel the world and some of us were meant to drill concrete. The title of your purpose doesn't matter; what matters is that it makes you happy. A daily sense of purpose trumps all the monetary riches in the world, and this purpose cannot be found in the opinions and beliefs of others—only you know this purpose.

External events don't define you

The Forever Youngs who walk this world mute the outside world and all of its opinions, ideas, and judgments. Even when surrounded by turmoil and despair, they seem to be unaffected, unharmed,

---

[1] https://www.ted.com/talks/steve_jobs_how_to_live_before_you_die.

and unburdened. Their inner flame always flickers, regardless of the issues that present themselves. These are individuals who view and handle problems differently than most. For example, most individuals catching a flight get frustrated if their plane is delayed. They moan about how poorly the airline is run and how all their activities and appointments will be delayed. They become angry, nervous, or sad. These feelings have lower vibrations, and this lower-vibration energy lingers with them, sometimes even ruining their entire trip.

Conversely, the Forever Youngs in this situation don't react immediately with anger or frustration. Instead, they see it as an opportunistic event. They know the plane will arrive when it arrives and not a second too late or too early. For them, the delay might be a chance to catch up on their reading, to mingle with other passengers, or to meditate or take a nap. In other words, they don't allow events outside their control to control them. And not only do they see the delay as purposeful and opportunistic—they also feel grateful for it. They are happy to be catching a flight in the first place, knowing that a few hundred years ago, getting from Calgary to Vancouver would take months. Higher-vibrating individuals see events through this kind of lens. They see the world in perfect order and harmony and don't allow anything to create lower-vibrating energies within them, for they know there is no value in being anything other than happy.

Your world can be perfect

Several years ago, I was listening to one of Wayne Dyer's audio books: *How to be a No-Limit Person.* Dyer is an author considered by many to be the father of motivation. This tape includes an interview that a young reporter conducted with a man named Nisargadatta Maharaj.

Essentially, the reporter asked him how he could be so full of love when the world around him was so dark. Maharaj paused for a moment and then responded gently, saying that in his world, all was exactly as it should be.

Maharaj wasn't implying that he didn't care what went on around him. Rather, he chose not to fill his mind with darkness, or become attached to such turmoil. He understood the power of our thoughts and how they can affect our world. Your reality reflects what you think about all day long; it has nothing to do with what goes on around you. He chose to fill his head with love rather than hate, and so he attracted things that made him feel loved.

We cannot attract more positive experiences into our lives by thinking about all the negative stuff that happens to us or around us. Ignore what the tribe is telling you and instead focus on cultivating your own reality through higher-functioning thoughts.

When you think about what you want, it will find you

A frame of mind that is built around problems rather than solutions will only create more problems. As Albert Einstein said, "We cannot solve our problems with the same level of thinking that created them." We cannot eradicate hate with more hate, but we can eradicate it by responding with love. We cannot become millionaires by constantly telling ourselves, "I can't afford that" or "I don't deserve that." Instead, we must think rich, think high level. We must feel that we deserve all the abundance in the world if we wish to attract prosperity. We need to shift away from the thoughts that create the shortfalls in our lives to higher-vibrating streams of thought. What we contemplate throughout the day will appear around us, as if by magic.

There will always be suffering, hate, and violence in the world if you look for it; there will always be people who are displeased with you if you look for them. What you search for will find you in abundance, whether it be love or hate. Majarah chose to see his world as a place filled with love, peace, and harmony, and this is what materialized for him. So many people choose to see the world through the lens of anger, bitterness, and negativity and are completely baffled when anger, bitterness, and negativity come knocking on their door. It's nothing but a choice. And in choosing to see the world as a place of love and joy rather than as place of hostility and hate, we not only become healthier human beings, but we also unconsciously spread that higher-level vibration to those around us.

Listen to your world, not the tribe

Again, there is only one person you should be listening to, and that person is you. When you look back on your life, there will be much regret if you followed what the tribe had in mind for you. Think about how many people have cheated themselves out of a better life because they didn't do what they wanted and instead stayed in a job they despised or an unhappy relationship. Think about how many people wake up every morning and say "Good god, it's morning" instead of "Good morning, God." Think about how many people put on a false personality to please those around them. Too many of us are watered-down versions of ourselves, and not enough of us are authentic, genuine, and vibrant.

The Forever Youngs would rather be authentic and criticized for who they are than inauthentic and loved by everyone. Others' plans for how you should live your life will never go as far as your plans for yourself. In other words, no one other than you has that knowing, that dream, that desire planted inside the fabric of his or her being. Only you know what you want out of life, and only you have what it takes to fully realize this desire. Don't let society control your divine expression. Every soul on this planet is here to express its individuality and talents through its own offerings and gifts. Remind yourself daily that you are here to live *your* life on *your* terms. Be you, be you, be you, and let go of tribal thinking.

How others treat you is their reality

If someone says something to you that is harsh, critical, or hurtful, take it lightly—how people respond to events reflects their own world.

Therefore, what they say and how they behave should have no bearing on your perception of yourself. Instead, see it as a glimpse into who they are. Their actions have everything to do with them and very little to do with you.

Wayne Dyer says that "you can't give what you don't have." In his *Power of Intention* lectures he often asks his audiences: "When you squeeze an orange, what comes out of it?" Not grapefruit or lemon juice but orange juice, of course. Why, you ask? Well, that's what's inside. Furthermore, it doesn't matter who or what is doing the squeezing. The same sweet liquid will come out of the orange, regardless. Dyer explains that we can relate this concept to life. When someone approaches you with negativity, and you respond the same way, you're doing so because that's what you hold inside. If you're filled with low-vibrating thoughts, that is exactly what will come out of you in times of stress.

You can't accept or give love if you have none for yourself. Those who respond with the low-vibrating emotions when "squeezed" operate in the realm of the Takers. They try to gain their power and strength (in order to feel better about themselves) through dominating, ridiculing, judging, and belittling others. As discussed earlier, the Takers' primary issue is a lack of self-love. They fill their inner emptiness by breaking others down. Instead of feeling attacked by these individuals, try to remember that they're responding or acting out according to how they feel inside.

Conversely, the Forever Youngs when "squeezed" release confidence, security, peacefulness, and openness. They see the tribe's opinions and beliefs as simply noise; it fails to penetrate their perception of themselves. These individuals make no time for judgmental or critical thoughts, which vibrate at a lower frequency and create disease in the body (more on this later). They also simply don't feel the need to extend judgment, for they understand that we're all doing the best we can given the stories of our lives. Next time someone approaches you with a judgment, ask yourself, "What's the subtext here?" In time, you'll begin to realize that what's being said is not about you but a reflection of that person's distressing world, and the "juices" they hold within.

A life spent trying to please the tribe will always elude you. There will always be someone who finds fault it what you`re doing. So, end your tireless search for approval for it will never fill your cup. As you work on leaving the tribe behind, you will pursue the things that resonate with you. You'll move in the direction of your own passions and your own dreams, for you will begin to see that you have no requirement to do what others expect of you. Nobody knows you better than you know yourself, so why listen to what others have in mind for you? Understanding this allows you to separate yourself from the tribe and the way they think and act. And once separated, you will begin to hear your own voice more clearly and rediscover that greatness within.

Affirmation

I know that in this life, there will always be a critic, no matter what I decide to do or express. I choose to live my life based on my inner reality, and I disregard the beliefs and opinions of others. What other people think of me is a reflection of their reality and where they are in their karmic paths. Life is but a moment in eternity, and I will not concern myself with external beliefs, opinions, and ideas, for this is my unique journey.

I am Forever Young

3

BE PLAYFUL

"This is the real secret of life—to be completely engaged with what you are doing in the here and now. And instead of calling it work, realize it is play."

-Alan Watts

It's true: the world in which we live is a playful one. A life full of laughter, wonder, joy, and adventure is our birthright. I was told from a young age to never lose my sense of playfulness, for playfulness is key to connecting with our essence. Children can teach us how to remain in this state of curiosity, for their minds are boundless, not confined by limiting beliefs. As children, we entered new worlds simply by using our imagination. Our days consisted of fairy-tale lands and make-believe stories and characters full of magic and mysticism. It's easy to lose our cheekiness when life hits hard with deadlines, duties, and dramas.

Taxes, bills, mortgages, car payments, loans, and the search for rewarding, progressive careers and relationships—all these things can take over that lighthearted, youthful spirit that resides within us. We strive for money and efficiency; we strive to be responsible. How many times have you heard the words "grow up" or "quit acting like a child"? Within our society exists the misconception that "childish" and "childlike" mean the same thing. But being childish is very different from being childlike. Being childlike means taking time out of your day to play with your partner or friends, daydream, fantasize, role play, sing, dance, laugh, and find joy in seemingly dull moments. To be childish is to be careless, immature, and irrational. One can be childlike and responsible at the same time.

It's one thing to say we should be more playful but much harder to actually put into practice.

However, the Forever Youngs work to maintain that level of playfulness and fun well into their last days. To remain Forever Young we must learn to laugh more, play more, and be more curious in nature. We should strive to carry those childlike attributes throughout our lives. In this chapter, we will learn to implement playfulness into our everyday world—because not only is being playful fun, more importantly, many physical, mental, and emotional benefits come from doing so.

Observe play

Through several studies, researchers have revealed that playfulness and kindness are therapeutic. Even the simple act of observing playfulness in others provokes a strong biological response. For example, watching two individuals playing a game of tag or hide-and-seek instantly triggers a chemical response in the observer's brain—high levels of serotonin (the neurotransmitter associated with pleasure and happiness) are released into the bloodstream. What's even more interesting is that the observer's brain actually secretes twice as much serotonin as those of the individuals involved in the play.[2] In

---

[2] http://undergroundhealthreporter.com/act-of-kindness/.

other words, observing playfulness in others elicits a stronger biological response than participating in play. So next time you feel down and out, make an effort to enjoy an activity or, better yet, to watch an activity that involves laughter and joy. You will literally create molecules in your brain that allow you to feel happier.

Get outside & play

When we observe the natural world, we can see that play is happening all the time. The trees stretch out to the sun in joy, the stars twinkle and dance in the night sky, and animals chase each other over the grass. Dogs play fetch, cats play hide-and-seek, and dolphins create games to play with each other. In fact, dolphins are considered one of the most playful mammals in the animal kingdom. These skillful swimmers take joy in shooting out of the water and performing acrobatic flips and spins. Countless surfers have spotted dolphins body surfing next to them while they ride the waves.[3] There is much we can learn from all of life's creatures. If they make time for play, why shouldn't we?

---

[3] http://www.dailymail.co.uk/video/news/video-1099862/Incredible-footage-dolphins-riding-waves-WA.html.

Playfulness keeps us young at heart and full of energy, so we must never lose sight of it. Take time each day to find a moment of laughter and excitement. All too often, we take life so darn seriously. Even death, which so many of us fear, is simply the universe playing hide-and-seek with our physical forms. We all come into the physical plane and then disappear into the divine. Death is a natural part of life that should not be feared. Think of life as just one giant, playful game of peekaboo that spans infinite time and space. Grasping this idea can provide a sense of relief; it can help us lighten up and let go of petty concerns. Make time each day to go outside and play, for in doing so, you will become a happier human being.

Reverse the effects of time

Several years ago, Dr. Ellen Langer, a psychologist at Harvard, published an experiment that demonstrates the importance of maintaining a youthful attitude throughout life.[4] In 1979, a group of senior citizens participated in her world-renowned study, which produced head-scratching results that redefined the concept of time. The study participants were taken to a monastery

---

[4] Ellen J. Langer, Counterclockwise: Mindful Health and the Power of Possibility (Ballantine Books, 2009).

renovated to reflect an atmosphere of the 1950s—the drapes, the TVs, the furniture, the light fixtures, and even the *TIME* magazines. When they turned the TVs on, participants could only watch programs that aired in the 1950s. Board games, colouring books, Lego sets, and all sorts of toys and devices were also placed purposefully throughout the monastery to reflect this period in time. The environment was designed to induce in participants memories of their adolescent years. The guideline participants were left with? Be as you were in the 1950s. Don't reminisce, but simply be as you were when you were in your twenties. With that, the researcher shut the monastery's doors and left the participants to mingle and coexist for two weeks. During this time, they had no contact with the outside world.

Something miraculous happened. What Dr. Langer discovered when the participants came to the lab two weeks later was nothing short of astonishing. Highly refined scans and sophisticated sampling techniques performed on each senior revealed that every single participant had reversed the biological markers of aging—not stopped or paused them, but literally reversed them! Their visual and hearing thresholds had improved, their systolic blood pressure had gone down, their skin had become more elastic with more fat underneath, causing their wrinkles to fade, their bone density had become thicker, and the levels of adrenal steroids (which control sex drive) had increased exponentially in their circulatory systems, thus improving their libidos. Everything Dr. Langer measured exemplified biological characteristics of a more youthful state: characteristics equivalent to that of a twenty-something-year-old. And these results occurred simply as a result of participants' living in an environment designed to bring about a more youthful and playful state. All Dr. Langer did was create a sensory-rich environment based on an earlier time period and tell participants to be as they were when they were young!

The big lesson here is simply this: our minds create our reality. If we see ourselves as young, confident, and capable, our bodies will respond to reflect this thinking. We need to think young to be young. And this concept applies to every aspect of our lives. If we want something, we need to feel as if we already have it; if we want to win, we must feel as if we have already won; if we want to be rich, we must feel as if we're already rich. The world will respond to who you think you are. What you think you are, you will eventually become. Walter D. Wintle, a nineteenth-century poet, powerfully expresses this idea in the following poem:

"Thinking"

If you think you are beaten, you are
If you think you dare not, you don't,
If you like to win, but you think you can't
It is almost certain you won't.

If you think you'll lose, you're lost
For out of the world we find,
Success begins with a fellow's will
It's all in the state of mind.

If you think you are outclassed, you are
You've got to think high to rise,
You've got to be sure of yourself before
You can ever win a prize.

Life's battles don't always go
To the stronger or faster man,
But soon or late the man who wins
Is the man who thinks he can!"

Celebrate each year that passes with grace and appreciation. Change how you think about growing old and begin to create realities that benefit your body, your world, and your soul. Think playful, think curious. And take joy in everything during your brief journey upon this planet, for this will create a happier and healthier you. This will allow you to be Forever Young.

Affirmation

I choose to live this life lightly, for I reside in a universe that is playful and recreational. I know my thoughts create my reality. Thus, I choose thoughts that help me to remain healthy and strong. I know that the cells in my body are a direct reflection of how I perceive the world. Therefore, I see myself as growing younger every day. Each day, my cells are replenished, repaired, and replaced. Each day they are in a healthier and more vital state. I am ageless, timeless, and full of positive thoughts.

I am Forever Young

4

LET GO OF YOUR BODY

Your body is just the place that your spirit calls home for the time being.

As Pierre Teilhard de Chardin said so eloquently, "We are not human beings having a spiritual experience. We are spiritual beings having a human experience." As a society, we are obsessed with the physical body and how to present it. We are infatuated with designer brands, silk thread counts, and how others perceive the outline of our body and colour of our skin. The clothes we wear—the way pieces of cloth fall upon our shoulders—often seem to be of the utmost importance. We are so fixated on how the world perceives us that we completely forget the life force that drives and animates our very existence: our soul. We are far greater than just a set of bones surrounded by fat, muscle, and skin. In truth, we are fields of energy infusing these vessels we call our bodies for a fraction of time in eternity. To be Forever Young, see yourself as something far grander than your body, which is limited and confined to its environment. The physical body lasts for only so long before it deteriorates into dust and is recycled in the soil. It is nothing more than the medium in which your spirit can express itself at this time.

A great teacher of mine once said that our bodies account for 1 percent of our form; the other 99 percent of who we are is invisible, untouchable, and impervious to the senses. Think about it: the body you reside in for years accounts for only 1 percent of your being! Truly remarkable. Don't you think we should be more concerned with the other 99 percent of our selves? The Forever Youngs understand the importance of nourishing and caring for their physical bodies but seek to understand and nourish the intangible, mystical side of their forms as well. The aim of this chapter is to allow you to live your life from that *'99 percent'* realm—the world of thought. Who we are, stems from the quality of our thinking. And if we can learn to create healthier and happier thoughts from within, our bodies and life will follow suit.

Time is limited

To be Forever Young, we must remember that life is short. One minute you're in your twenties and the next, you're in your sixties reminiscing about how enjoyable high school and university was. I'd bet my bottom dollar that for many of you, it feels like just yesterday you were roaming the halls, shooting spitballs at teachers, and playing basketball on your high school's courts. But time waits for no one, and we all share that common destination in the end. We all grow old. That perfectly sculpted body will wear out and wear thin until it powers off.

Let's reflect on the idea of mortality for a moment—great wisdom is gained in doing so. The thought of death scares most of us, and this fear makes us turn a blind eye to the idea that someday, we will leave this world behind. So instead of thinking about this, we get caught up in life's daily routines. Often it's not until we are terminally sick or on our deathbeds that we begin to really understand what's important to us. The simple act of thinking of our own death changes the way we live almost instantly. Consider this: on average, about two hundred thousand people die each day—that's roughly 70 million people per year. But don't let this statistic make you feel despair. Instead, let it free you from the fear of death. Once we appreciate that we won't live forever, we can begin to make time for the things that matter to us, and to pursue what we desire. We have only so many breaths, so why wouldn't we spend our days—spend our lives—following our excitement?

The Floaters often have a hard time understanding that our time on earth is limited. They tend to go through life without a sense of purpose or direction, as if they have all the time in the world to do what they want, when they want. The Floaters do their essence a great disservice. They are what I like to call the sleepwalkers: they are here physically but have checked out mentally, emotionally, and spirituality. The 99 percent of their existence is dormant, stifled, and unfulfilled. They have not yet nourished their souls; their meaning has yet to be discovered.

Remember: we have only so many heartbeats and hours to find that purpose within us. With that, don't let fear keep you from doing the things you want to do. Why not ask that special person out on that date? Why not push yourself to become better and try that thing that's scary? Why not do that thing you've been putting off for so long now? We all end up in a wooden box six feet underground anyway. Take risks, explore the unknown, follow your intuition. Live, don't float. It's far better to end your life battered and bruised with purpose than to arrive safely and unscathed but without fulfillment. Our names will be forgotten, our physical bodies will perish, and the world will continue to spin without us.

To be Forever Young, find that which fills your soul. Maybe for you that means starting a company, adopting a child, or working at the fish market. Anything that gives you bliss, excitement, and a sense of purpose in your everyday life will allow you to reconnect with your essence.

Who you are, not what you have

So many people define their self-worth by their careers, their physiques and the material possessions they accumulate over a lifetime. When your happiness is dependent on the external world, the external world is in control, not you. There is more to life and more to your purpose than just collecting material goods, having that perfectly sculpted face, and being able to define yourself as a banker, painter, dancer, or writer. It is far more valuable to collect memories and friendships, for these things are timeless, boundless, and infinite. Possessions, your body, and careers are not.

Look around and you'll see numerous individuals justifying their existence in the following ways: "I am an MVP"; "I am a welder"; "I am an analyst"; "I am a lifeguard"; "I am an accountant"; "I am a banker." The labels we place on ourselves are superficial and fleeting. We won't always be the MVP, the welder, the analyst, or the lifeguard. We won't always live on the corner lot of Sunset Boulevard and we won't always have money. Everything we "have" in this lifetime is part of a rental agreement we made with the universe. We are temporarily acting as the banker, the welder, or the analyst, until the next person in line comes along and takes the position. I can assure you that after your time on this planet has expired, you will not be remembered for where you lived or what car you drove—you will be remembered for how you made others feel, which is what's everlasting in this world.

If we associate who we are with what we have, then what happens if we lose these things? What do we become? Well, if our self-worth is tied to a possession and that possession disappears, we essentially become worthless and unenviable. Sadly, self-worth is so often tied to possessions in this way, and thus insecurity and self-doubt are big issues for many people. If you rely on the external to validate your existence, your cup will never be full. You will always want more. So instead, remind yourself on a regular basis that you are valuable, sacred, and precious simply because you exist. Quit being so hard on yourself and comparing yourself to others, for we are all on unique journeys and we all have unique karmic missions.

It's time that you perceived and treated yourself with compassion and love. Think of it this way: if you found something of incredible value, you would work hard to keep it in pristine condition, right? Well, you are of incredible value. Nourish your body with healthy foods, healthy thoughts, and healthy practices. You are incredibly, uniquely, fantastically special and valuable because you're a piece of the divine. All the riches in the world couldn't buy your energy, your character, and your soul. Begin to see yourself as valuable and rich, not because of what you have, but because of who you are as a person, and you will be Forever Young.

Connecting with yourself through nature

On a molecular level, we are all made up of the same stuff. 5 There are only so many elements that form the visible universe. Carbon, hydrogen, oxygen, and nitrogen (CHON) are the building blocks of life. Humans appear different from trees, plants from animals, rocks from water, etc. because the same elements are arranged in slightly different ways. Everything and everyone comes from the same rudimentary physical elements on the periodic table. Even the stars you see twinkling in the night sky, so great and grand, the nebulas and galaxies billions of light years away, consist of the same ingredients that make up our skin, bones, tissue, teeth, and hair. We are CHON and they are CHON. Carl Sagan once said, "Our planet, our society, and we ourselves are built of star stuff." He meant this quite literally. Consider this the next time you gaze upon the stars. When we see the external world and all its beauty, what we are really seeing is a reflection of ourselves. A beautiful thought indeed. We must rekindle our connection with nature, for we are not separate from this environment—we have been born from it. We are

---

[5] http://www.phschool.com/science/biology_place/biocoach/biokit/chnops.html.

much grander than the bodies in which we live. We are intrinsically connected to the environment around us.

Connecting with nature is connecting with our essence. Nature keeps us grounded and in the present moment. It reminds us of our true origin, the one uninterrupted by life's nuisances. It keeps us Forever Young. Nature is not filled with the worries of tomorrow. Nature is silent, it is still, it just is. When we are in nature we become silent, we become still, we can just be. Spend time with this calming energy unburdened by troubles, deadlines, and meetings. It is a living and breathing being, just like you. Stroll in the park alone or with family or friends. Run your hands through the grass or the sand. Stop and smell the flowers. Close your eyes and tune in to your sense of hearing—listen to birds, leaves in the wind, or other sounds you'd otherwise miss. Watch the sunset or focus on a tiny part of nature, a leaf or single blade of grass. Take breaks from whatever you're doing and go outside. You'll likely return refreshed and refocused.

What's next?

Whether you believe in reincarnation or not, there is one thing we can all agree on—at some point, our bodies will leave this world behind.

They will decompose into the earth. Again, it's important to acknowledge this truth; it will help you to appreciate the time you are given here and to use it purposefully, strategically, and graciously. With that, let's take a closer look at the physical process of death.

Minutes after the body's death, cells and tissues, lacking necessary oxygen, begin to die off. Bacteria within the body breaks the cells down into smaller and smaller particles. The body takes on a ghastly appearance, and the decomposing tissues emit gases such as methane and hydrogen fluoride. Bacteria will feed on the decaying flesh until what was once a body becomes microscopic particles enriching the soil with nutrients necessary for the growth of all life. What was once a living human is recycled in the earth to become indistinguishable from the surrounding soil. This imagery is graphic, but I use it to help you disconnect from your physical body.

Now that your body has "perished," ask yourself these very important questions:

Where is my essence now?
Where is "me"?

What's next?

Where do I go now?

Who am I now?

Where is my value?

These questions have mystified humans for centuries. Death and the afterlife have always baffled us. Along with these questions, consider the poem "Reincarnation," written by Wallace McRae. [6] He makes the sobering point that when it's all said and done, you're essentially a pile of animal dung. From a physical perspective there is much truth to this, for animal dung has the same cellular components as our bodies. But from a spiritual perspective, the reality is vastly different. Your essence, your soul, your vibes, your chi—whatever you want to call it—has moved on. It is certainly not residing in that dung. Yes, our bodies perish and become one with the earth upon death. However, our essence continues. It continues to take on other forms. We weep and despair when loved ones pass away, but we must remember that only their physical form has died; their energy, their spirit, their essence can never perish: it is

---

[6] http://www.cowboypoetry.com/mcrae.htm.

everlasting. What organizes your very life, your very being, your very existence, is beyond the physical. It is infinite. Many people see mediums and psychics in order to connect with the energy of those who have passed over, for this energy is still very much present. The body may have dissolved into the earth, but the soul remains. Consider Mary Elizabeth Frye's poem "Do Not Stand at My Grave and Weep," [7] which sums up this idea beautifully.

To be Forever Young, acknowledge that what constitutes your existence is not the body but the energy that gives rise to your body.

You are your energy

Everything in the universe is made up of energy, and this energy is measured in vibrations. Positive thoughts create positive vibrations, and positive vibrations gyrate quickly. Conversely, negative thoughts create negative vibrations, and negative vibrations gyrate slowly. If you were to look at an atom under a powerful microscope, you would see mostly empty space surrounded by vibrating electrons, protons, and neutrons. Quantum physics is beginning to reveal that atoms are not material in nature but simply vibrations emitting electrical

[7] https://www.poemhunter.com/poem/do-not-stand-at-my-grave-and-weep/.

impulses. These impulses can be observed and quantified with sophisticated particle-detection technology. And astonishingly, these impulses can manipulate the speed of neighbouring atoms' vibrations. So, if an atom is emitting weak, slow impulses, nearby atoms will begin to do the same. So what, you ask? Well, understanding this concept is imperative to reaching higher levels of consciousness. The human body is made up of atoms. Thus, the vibrations we give off can have a profound impact not only on us, but also on those around us. Whether we are aware of it or not, we pick up on these impulses all the time.

Have you ever met with someone only to feel immediately anxious or sick? Have you ever felt a sense of sadness or intrusion before someone has uttered even a single word? This is your energetic field interacting with another's, and you are registering the level of consciousness at which that person is operating. You are picking up on their bad vibes, the thoughts they are carrying with them. And have you ever met with someone and instantly felt a sense of excitement, joy, and love? This person is likely a Forever Young radiating high-frequency energy and thus raising your own energy level. Trust your instincts when you meet with people or go to places; everything emits a frequency. What you surround yourself with affects your field all the time, so it's very important to surround yourself with people and places that empower you.

If you find yourself carrying around low-vibrating energy, consider something a dear mentor once told me— *"If you cannot enjoy your life in some way, shape, or form, you are not only a burden to yourself but also a burden to those around you."* No amount of negative thinking will ever brighten this world; it will only darken it. Enjoy your life, for this enjoyment will positively affect the world around you. No words or actions are needed. Simply shift your internal dialogue from disempowering to empowering and see how the world responds to your conscious mind's thinking.

Your body responds to thoughts

When Western methods of treatment are combined with Eastern ones, disease and illness in the body can often be cured. Western medicine tends to focus on symptoms, while Eastern medicine aims to understand where the disease originated. If we want long-term healing to take place in our bodies, we must first approach illness from an Eastern perspective. Eastern philosophies tend to promote the idea that all ailments can be traced back to a single negative thought—a thought that originated from you and no one else. Therefore, if we are willing to put in the mental effort to discover what sort of internal dialogue created the ailment in the first place, we can begin our journey to perfect health. In her powerful book *You Can Heal Your Life*, Louise Hay discusses the mind-body connection in detail. Her premise is that every thought we hold expresses itself as a specific symptom in the body. For example:

Unsettled stomach – fear of the unknown

Skin sores – unexpressed and unresolved anger

Vision issues – not liking what you see in your life

Anxiety – not trusting that everything in life shows up exactly on time; feeling as if there is not enough time in the day [8]

Because every thought affects the body, we need to be mindful of what we're allowing to circulate in our minds. Thoughts of love produce atoms that vibrate in harmony with one another; thoughts of hate produce the opposite. Therefore, if we can

---

[8] Louise Hay, You Can Heal Your Life (Hay House, 1984), p. 192.

manifest illness through our thoughts, we can also manifest healing and health. To address the physical issues that arise in my body, I look at the symptom list Hay presents in *You Can Heal Your Life* and counter the symptom with my own affirmations:

Unsettled stomach – "I choose to have a mind that is open to new situations and circumstances."

Skin sores – "It's okay to be angry; I can express my anger in joyous and positive ways."

Vision issues – "I know that I am the creator of my life, and I choose to attract that which I desire."

Anxiety – "I am on an infinite journey through life. I am at ease, and I trust that everything and everyone is revealed to me exactly on time and on purpose. All is as it should be."

While these affirmations are quite specific, you don't need an extensive list of targeted affirmations to treat each misalignment within your body. You just need to shift your internal dialogue to that of a higher vibration. Change thoughts of victimization, hate, blame, regret, anger, and hostility to thoughts of acceptance, nonjudgment, respect, admiration, excitement, and hope. It's that simple. The Forever Youngs not only care for their bodies through healthy eating and exercise—they also work at taking caring of their minds. They work to ensure that constructive, empowering thoughts are filling their consciousness. As Lao Tzu said, "If you correct your mind, the rest of your life will fall into place." Learn to love yourself and feed your mind with nourishing thoughts; your world will respond accordingly.

Unconsciousness sickness

Many people wonder why they continue to experience the same sickness time and time again, despite having been prescribed medication and given a treatment plan. By now, you probably understand that the mind plays an important role in healing. The issue lies in the thought that created the sickness in the first place. So if we experience the same sickness again and again, it's because we keep thinking the same detrimental thoughts again and again. Misaligned thinking could be manifesting itself as that hacking cough, that pesky ulcer, that constant fever, or that high blood pressure. "Subconscious" illness is much more difficult to resolve, for it is a result of an ingrained belief—perhaps one that has been carried since childhood.

Most of us are completely unaware of unresolved childhood issues. When we live for many years with certain beliefs, we become accustomed to and thus unaware of them. For example, perhaps you've lived with the thought "I'm not good enough" from a very young age. Your father or your mother may have scolded you, day in, day out, saying things such as "You disappoint me," "I can't stand you," or "Why can your friends do this better than you?" While you may not remember the dialogue, the energy of a conversation like this can work its way into your very being. And to compensate for such a belief, you try to prove yourself to others. You try to be the best at everything to protect yourself from ever hearing those words again.

These kinds of issues can be brought to the surface only through deep reflection. We must do the work to discover the negative mental chatter within us. And once we shift the negative belief to a positive one, in this case "I'm not good enough" to "I'm more than good enough," that pesky cough or sore throat will fade away, as if by magic. What illness is constantly recurring in your life? Sit down with yourself and dive deep to find the dialogue creating that cycle within you. Once you uncover that negative chatter, you can treat those illnesses that hide beneath the radar.

Your body can heal itself

Now that we've determined that positive thoughts can contribute to a healthy life, let's look at a real-life example. Medical professionals typically encourage individuals with kidney cancer to purchase vials of interleukin as a form of treatment. Interleukin helps the immune system fight abnormal cell growth. These vials can cost thousands of dollars each and can quickly cause crushing debt. However, our bodies can create the same hormone naturally.

In Deepak Chopras lecture, *Living Beyond Miracles* he discusses the powerful relationship between our thoughts/experiences and the body; and that when we practice seeing the world as opportunistic and joyful, what we are really practicing is body chemistry. For example, researchers separated individuals with kidney cancer (in the same stage) into two groups: Group A and Group B. For one month, the individuals in Group A were exposed to fun. They were sent to amusement parks around the world, where they rode roller coasters and Ferris wheels, drove bumper cars, and plummeted down drop rides. Blood samples were extracted before and after each amusement park session to assess interleukin levels within the participants' bloodstreams. What the researchers discovered was remarkable. A one-week trip to the amusement park resulted in the secretion of thousands and thousands of dollars worth of interleukin. The individuals in Group B were not exposed to any elements of fun, and their interleukin levels remained at the baseline level throughout the entire experiment. So, can our bodies produce other "drugs" to fight other illness? The answer is yes, of course. The interleukin experiment further shows that we are not our bodies; we are the awareness behind them. Furthermore, it demonstrates that what we think about and how we see the world not only impacts the chemistry of the brain, but the body as well.

I've seen firsthand that reflecting on the thought of love and love alone, which is the highest-vibrating energy in the cosmos, can cure the worst diseases known to humankind. If we can learn to love ourselves unconditionally, we can rid any deficiency within ourselves. Be very mindful of what you think about throughout the day, for thoughts fuelled by anger, hatred, bitterness, resentment, and spite provide feeding grounds for dysfunctional cells. Instead, reflect on gratitude, love, courage, hope, second chances, youthfulness, flexibility, and fun. You will vibrate at a higher frequency and experience a healthy body, mind, and spirit. Again, we are not our bodies but the accumulation of what we think about all day long. The body is but a mere reflection of the conscious mind.

We outlive our cells

I've heard many people disregard the philosophy that healthy thoughts create a healthy body. They argue that they're genetically predisposed to illness and therefore, their thoughts have no bearing on their health. What I say to these individuals is that we are reborn all the time—the argument doesn't hold up.

Every single day, new cells replace old cells in our bodies. There are trillions upon trillions of cells within us, and each of these cells contributes to a different function and purpose. Carbon dating and radioactive isotope studies conducted at the Oak Ridge Atomic Research Center show that different cells in the body are replaced at different rates. For example, the turnover time (fully replaced with new cells) of the stomach is two to nine days; the small intestine, two to four days; the cervix, six days; the trachea, roughly sixty days, and so on. Though the body may seem dense and stationary, it is in a constant state of movement and change. In fact, within seven years, every single cell in your body will have died off and been replaced with new cells. Even your bones, which seem so hard and solid, will be entirely new. Who you were seven years ago is extinct! Knowledge of this simple fact should eliminate all excuses related to past performance and illness. "I was born with it," "I'm not smart enough," "I failed the last time I tried it," "I was never good at tennis"—toss them all out the window, for your body is redefining itself every single day.

You may be wondering, "Well if I'm a completely new person, why do I still have a sore throat? Or arthritis? Or high blood pressure? And why am I still bad at tennis?" While you may be a completely new person in regards to your cell structure, your thoughts have yet to change. And if your thoughts have yet to change, the same genetic tendencies will appear over and over again within the body. You're not reinventing yourself—you're replicating your past. You have not treated the root cause of the illness. You are still thinking low-frequency thoughts, and your body is creating new cells that mirror these thoughts. Your negative mental chatter serves to keep you stuck in that low-vibrating sickness.

I'll say it again: the way we perceive ourselves affects our vibrational state, and our vibrational state has a wide-reaching impact on not only our own well-being, but also on the world around us.

To wrap up this chapter, here's an excerpt from *A New Earth: Awakening to Your Life's Purpose.* Eckhart Tolle discusses how we are so fixated on our bodies (our forms) that we have forgotten that very force that animates our existence:

"The collective disease of humanity is that people are so engrossed in what happens, so hypnotized by the world of fluctuating forms, so absorbed in the content of their lives, they have forgotten the essence, that which is beyond content, beyond form, beyond thought. They are so consumed by time that they have forgotten eternity, which is their origin, their home, their destiny. Eternity is the living reality of who you are." [9]

---

[9] Eckhart Tolle, A New Earth: Awakening to Your Life's Purpose (Penguin Books, 2008) p. 65.

To be Forever Young, we must not get caught up in the physicality of the world. Our bodies are merely vessels in which are soul calls home for the time being. Let go your fixation for appearances, possessions, and titles for these things are temporary and fleeting. Instead, shift your focus to the 99 percent realm, for that is where living can truly take place.

Affirmation

I know that I am an energetic being encapsulating a body and that what constitutes my existence is beyond my physical form. I am what I choose to think about all day long, so I choose to think healthy thoughts that create good vibes within me. My cells are constantly being replaced and replenished, so the past has no bearing on my current state of affairs. From this moment forward I choose to experience high-vibrating energies that contribute to a life of perfect health.

I am Forever Young

5

QUIT WORRYING

"Life isn't as serious as the mind makes it out to be."

-Eckhart Tolle

Lighten up, relax, enjoy the scenery — and quit worrying about everything! It's easy to get caught up in the drama of our everyday lives, but let's put things into perspective. Consider this passage from the Bible: "For we have brought nothing into the world, and it is certain we can carry nothing out." [10] We enter this world with no possessions: no cell phones, no money, no

---

[10] Timothy 6:7–12 (King James Version)

mortgage, no suitcases, no clothes, no movie collections, nothing. We show up naked, helpless, and crying, and our lives often end in a similar fashion. Then we're put into a coffin, our assets are divided, our bank accounts are closed, and we dry up into dust that the earth recycles. It's as plain and simple as that.

So why do we put so much stress, sweat, and tears into accumulating goods? Into making an impression? Into people pleasing? Why are we so distraught when we miss those deadlines, or when we're five minutes behind schedule? Why do we allow traffic jams to ruin our day? Why do we get so frustrated when the line at the grocery store has more than five people in it or someone in the express lane is two items over the ten-item limit? And why is it when we discover that the shirt we wanted to buy is out of stock, we act as if it's the end of the world?

We human beings can be overdramatic, inclined to feel as if we're starring in a soap opera. But it is our true nature to be stress free, calm, and relaxed. Anxiety, anger, depression, and fear are unnatural ways of being. Joy is our birthright, and we were placed on this earth to experience it and share it with others.

When we fixate on the petty concerns of the day, our thinking becomes small and restricted. To overcome these minuscule matters, we need to put our attention on the big picture. Let lineups, flat tires, and lousy meals roll off your back like water. It's time to stop being so dramatic about what's irrelevant and time to start enjoying the things that are timeless, boundless, and forever.

The fact of the matter is that one day you and all your possessions will be gone, so why worry who has what? No amount of worrying will change the fact that everything physical perishes. After your death, people will keep getting their Tim Hortons coffee, eating dinner, playing video games, and accumulating goods. In other words, life will go on without you. So why put so much energy into worrying about what others have? Your presence, your soul, your energy, and how you made others feel—these things will be remembered. You won't be remembered for your home, your car, or how much stuff sat in your garage.

Growing your own garden

Instead of focusing on growing our own gardens, so many of us peep at the neighbours' yard, to see what they planted for themselves. What did they choose as a career? What kind of car did they buy? At what age did they marry? What kind of clothes do they wear? How much money do they make? Who are their friends? What do they watch? What kind of makeup do they wear? What did they post on Instagram or Snapchat?

To be Forever Young, stop comparing yourself and worrying about what the tribe has. We're all simply borrowing our material goods until our time here is up and these goods exchange hands. So, does it really matter who has more drywall or steel around their heads? Sure, a nice house (and garden!) is great to have, but the key is not to become obsessed with having one, or distraught because you don't have one. Comparison is a vicious circle that never ends; there will always be someone with more. Someone will always be richer, someone will always have a bigger house, someone will always get better grades, someone will always have more muscle, someone will always be more educated. Someone will always be prettier, bigger, smaller. What others have and how they live their lives is their business, not yours. Worry and comparison is pointless.

Stop being that pesky neighbour who's always worrying about what's happening on the other side of the fence; unplug from social media and close the blinds. If we keep focusing on what others are planting, we'll miss out on all the beauty and joy in our own backyards. And if you keep peeping at your neighbours' garden, you may discover (from being so pesky) that you've created a garden just like theirs and that it wasn't the one you envisioned for yourself. Cultivate your own life, your own garden, for it's uniquely yours. It's intended to be cared for by you and only you, without the neighbourhood's opinion.

Worrying makes no sense

Many of us create worry because we take everything too seriously. We obsess about controlling events and outcomes. But this desire for control creates huge amounts of pressure. We set goals and become so attached to creating a specific result that we make ourselves sick just thinking about it. We lose the fun in getting there.

To be Forever Young, enjoy the process of setting goals and appreciate the path set out before you. Be confident that you possess all the necessary tools and equipment to make the desired outcome a reality. Why worry when you have total control over your destiny? And when you have a Forever Young mindset, if for some reason something doesn't work out, you understand that it wasn't meant to be. The Forever Youngs know that worrying is a useless feeling that serves no purpose to their well-being.

Consider Wayne Dyer's view on worry from his book titled *Excuses Begone:* "First, it makes no sense to worry about the things you have control over, because if you have control over them, it makes no sense to worry about them. Second, it makes no sense to worry about the things you don't have control over, because if you can't control them, it makes no sense to worry about them." And there goes everything that it is possible to worry about. If you're worried about filing your taxes, get them done; if you're worried about gaining weight, exercise and eat better. And if you're worried about something you have no power over, it will happen regardless of what you do. Are you going to worry about going bald? No matter how many pills you pop or how many different ways you style your hair, it's going to happen. So why worry about it? Accept it and move on. Let go of the things you don't have control over and exert power over the things you do.

Quit being a burden and quit being the star in the soap opera of your life. Life doesn't need to be dramatic. Worrying is irrational, useless, and toxic.

Mark Twain once said, "I am an old man and have known many troubles, but most of them have never happened." When you think back on all the things you worried about, you'll find that most, if not all of them, never came to fruition, did they? You simply anticipated that something *might* go wrong.

Quit overanalyzing. Quit walking on eggshells because you're afraid of making a mistake or looking silly. Quit putting off your goals for the sake of staying comfortable. And quit being afraid of how others might see you. All of these things just create worry in your life. And worrying serves no purpose in your advancement. The universe is incredibly vast, and in the grand scheme of life, your worries and problems are incredibly small, despite how large and important they may appear. Life is much too short and valuable to focus our attention on life's little nuisances. As Paulo Coelho writes in *The Alchemist,* "We are travelers on a cosmic journey, stardust, swirling and dancing in the eddies and whirlpools of infinity. Life is eternal. We have stopped for a moment to encounter each other, to meet, to love, to share. This is a precious moment. It is a little parenthesis in eternity." [11]

---

[11] Paulo Coelho, The Alchemist (HarperTorch, Year), p. 32.

Life is but a flash, a speck. It goes by quickly, and the older we get, the more quickly it goes. Don't waste this "parenthesis in eternity" worrying. I've spoken with many people in their senior years, and most say the same thing: "It feels like yesterday I was in my twenties." Before you know it, you'll be eighty-five and playing bocce ball in a senior's home with your best bud from elementary school. Therefore, it's crucial to let go of the small stuff. Let go of the toxic relationship without worrying about the aftermath. Pursue a meaningful career without worrying about leaving your old one behind. Go back to school without worrying about whether you're too old—for life will continue to tick on, and "What if?" is the last question you want to cross your mind at the end of your life. Pursue what resonates with you.

Forever Youngs know that it's up to them to make something of their lives, to enjoy it and to live freely. Remember, the crowd too will perish into dust and the world will keep on spinning with or without your worrisome thoughts.

Thinking big dissolves worry

Do you ever wonder what lies beyond this planet? Do you wonder if other life-forms exist? Other dimensions? Other spiritual realms? Do you think about how vast the universe is? Or do you simply ponder what lies within your world? It's easy not to think about the big questions when we're caught up in the daily concerns of our lives, when we're trapped in the grind of nine-to-five and living for that two-day weekend. It's easy to forget that reality is magical, marvellous, and miraculous, to forget the beauty and mysticism this world has to offer.

To keep your worries at bay, think about this for a moment. The planet we inhabit is a piece of dust hurtling around a massive fireball at a speed of a thousand kilometres an hour—in a universe that extends forever. Pretty magical, huh? The earth has been around for about 5 billion years, and the human race has existed for only a few thousand. In the grand timeline of evolution, human life is merely a blink. Let this thought inspire gratitude and excitement. Let it put your worrisome thoughts into perspective. Most of them are trivial.

There are billions of other planets out among the nebulas, all with their own fireballs and orbital systems. Just looking into outer space from your living room window can be incredibly therapeutic—a reminder that there is something greater out there. We get so caught up in worrying about celebrities, the weather, and who wore what and on what day that we forget that there are whole other worlds beyond our speck of dust. Grasping this idea can help us see that we tend to view our lives through a confined lens and place importance on ridiculous matters most of the time. We worry about if our team will make the playoffs, we worry about spilling juice on our shirt, we worry about the forecast. We worry, we worry, we worry. You are a small bacterial organism held down by an invisible force called gravity residing on this tiny blue dot called Earth. Small, small, small. Get over your worries. The rest of the universe doesn't care about what you wore on Tuesday and if it was ironed or not. It's time to be Forever Young: get out of your own head, stop taking life so seriously, and adopt a big-picture frame of mind. Forever Youngs don't get bogged down with the everyday chatter of the world. They take delight in thinking big: the type of thinking that advances humanity into health and happiness.

You deserve to rest your busy mind and refocus your attention on the important things in life. Relationships, love, inspiration, and following your desires—these are things that really matter. Decide not to be that pesky neighbour who worries about what the person over the fence is or isn't planting.

Embrace the idea that worry serves no purpose, and you will surely create happiness in your life.

Affirmation

I choose to walk this earth lightly with a carefree spirit, for worrying serves no purpose to my well being. It is my birthright to be joyous and happy, so I work at filling my mind with thoughts that allow me to feel this way. I choose to spend my time cultivating my own garden without concern for the tribe's ideas and opinions. This is my unique path that I have chosen, so I live it according to my terms and conditions.

I am Forever Young

6

TRUST THE TIMING OF YOUR LIFE

You are always in the right place at the right time.

Everything that comes into our lives arrives exactly on time, not a second early nor a second late. Every person, every tribulation, every lover, every song on the radio—everything. From sitting beside a stranger in the movie theatre to meeting the love of your life on the train, every event is part of the perfection. Forever Youngs understand that events don't happen by accident or fluke. The universe creates everything with an intention.

This can be a difficult concept to grasp. You might be thinking about all the bad things that have happened in your life and asking yourself, "Were they really part of the perfect plan? How could these things possibly have occurred for my higher good? Was I really in the right place at the right time?" Time and time again, I will answer, "Yes, you were exactly where you should have been." The hardships, the deaths, the suffering, and the failures—it's all necessary. The world is providing you with tests for growth. Yes, life gives tests, and like tests we receive in school, if we fail life's tests, we must do them over and over again, until we attain a passing grade. Some of life's tests are harder than others, but they're all designed to propel us to higher levels of consciousness.

Life's tests

What do these tests prepare us for? They teach us to become individual thinkers, to be contributing members of society; they teach us how to grow, to persevere, and to become fully functioning human beings. We each have specific lessons to learn in this lifetime, and these lessons usually come in the form of adversity. Instead of seeing your life as one problem after another, begin to see that the universe is providing you with the necessary tools and skills to reach a higher level of awareness. Sure, you can complain about these problems all you want. OR you can choose to not be a victim and instead ask yourself, "What's the lesson in this? What is it that I need to learn in this very moment? What is the world trying to teach me?" Once you can see the problem as just a lesson from the universe, a universe that wants to shape you into the person you were destined to become, you can relax and enjoy the process without becoming addicted to the drama. It is as simple as that.

Unfortunately, most of us experience the troublesome events (tests) in our lives with regret, shame, sadness, anger, and despair. It's easy to get so caught up in what's happening that we fail to realize that what we're experiencing as a problem is just a stepping stone for advancement. It bears mentioning again: the breakups, the abusive relationships, the lack of money, the dysfunctional parents, the heartbreaks, the resentment, the problem children—all of it shows up exactly on time, and each problem contains something valuable for you to recognize. These tests are not always obvious, as the universe sometimes presents them in clever disguises. But more often than not, when we look back at certain hardships years down the road we can clearly see why we had to go through them. That devastating breakup could have been a lesson in independence, in learning to rely on yourself rather than your significant other. It could have been a lesson in self-love, in learning that you are valuable and worthwhile no matter what people say or do. It could have been a lesson in resilience, in learning how to persevere when the going gets tough without relying on others for support.

Whatever growing pains you may be going through at this very moment, know that every event in our world, no matter how tragic, serves as a catalyst for change and growth so that we may become more fully functioning human beings.

We came from intention

Have you ever thought about where you came from? The fact that a microscopic drop of protoplasm meeting with an egg creates life as we know it is perplexing enough to contemplate. In this miraculous moment, when the two elements make contact, the blueprint of your world begins. The shape and colour of your eyes, the pigment of your skin, how long your hair will stay in your head, your height—everything that you will become physically is contained within that tiny little cell. But what's even more perplexing is this: where did the egg and protoplasm come from? Mom and Dad, of course, but what brought them into existence? Before humans ever existed, where were we? What did we do? What were our personalities? Our goals? Our desires? Well the simple answer is that we've all come from that essence we discussed earlier. Everything and everyone comes from this place—every person, every bird, every blade of grass, and every mote of dust. I like to call it the Field of Forever Young, or Pure Happiness. Others call it Heaven, the afterlife (or beforelife), and/or the divine. Regardless of what you call it, we all stemmed from it; we all have the same roots, the same foundation, the same beginning. This field of energy from which we originated is pure perfection, pure love, and pure potential. It creates nothing by accident or fluke. Therefore, what comes into your life does not come by chance but by divine intention.

If we came from a place that has intended for us to be here, and this place is full of happiness and love, then whatever we're experiencing in our lives right now is designed to lead us to happiness and love. Coincidences don't exist—only purposeful encounters. The universe is always striving to help you be the best possible version of yourself, and if you must endure pain and suffering to be this better version, then that is exactly what the universe will allow you to experience. Life's difficulties are not here to discourage you but to empower you. When we connect with this notion that everything that shows up in our lives has a divine purpose, we begin to see the world in a different light. We see it as a Forever Young. We feel a sense of restfulness and bliss and begin to take the trials and tribulations more lightly. Instead of feeling victimized, upset, or angry, we see the silver lining. Again, the so-called issues in life are nothing more than blessings and tests disguised as troublesome events.

You signed up for it

I can already hear your thoughts racing: "Well, my mother sure in hell isn't here for my best interests," or "My dad definitely wasn't designed to bring out the best in me—in fact, he brought out the worst in me." However, I can assure you that if you have a difficult relationship with your parents, they are exactly what you need or needed. Love them or hate them, they are your guides in the lessons you chose to experience in this life. Let me explain: before you arrived here in this life, you made an agreement with the universe. And before making this agreement, you had a pretty serious conversation in regards to what you wanted to experience during your lifetime.

Some of you signed up to understand independence, and thus you were given parents who perhaps did little to support you financially, mentally, and physically so you could learn how to be self-reliant. This is just one example, of course. Different lessons require different people to come in and out of our lives. It's important to look at the difficult people in our lives not with bitterness or anger, but with gratitude. The people we find the most challenging to deal with are often those who have the greatest lessons to teach us. We come across these individuals throughout our time here to learn valuable things about ourselves.

The funny thing is, we will continue to come across these individuals until we learn from them (like the tests we talked about earlier). For example, let's say you keep attracting dysfunctional relationships. You change partners or friends, but no matter where you go, it's as if you keep running into the same person. The problems you had in past relationships follow you into the next chapter of your life to become problems in your current relationship. You date the same person or encounter the same friend, but in a different body, over and over again. The reason why you're experiencing this toxic relationship again and again is simple: you have not learned the required lesson. The universe will give you the same exam until a sufficient grade is achieved. It may be a lesson on letting go of possessiveness, trusting others, setting boundaries for yourself, or discovering how to be independent. Whatever the lesson may be, it is uniquely yours to learn. The next time you encounter someone or something that causes you grief, remember that the experience is but a gift from the universe—a gift intended to help you grow and advance, and move towards your higher truth.

I hope you are starting to see that the people who come into your life serve your life's story. I hope you are becoming more receptive to the idea that the tribulations in your life are purposeful and intentional. Perhaps the next time that little old man cuts in front of you on the highway, you'll smile instead of curse, even if he's driving thirty kilometres under the speed limit. Instead of immediately feeling anger and hostility, perhaps you'll shift your mentality. Maybe he's here to teach you to slow down and that there's more to life than making it go faster. Slow down, relax, enjoy the view, and be grateful that your car is running. The Forever Youngs see all the events in their lives, from the smallest to the largest, as stemming from a place of perfection and purpose, and therefore they embrace wholeheartedly what comes their way, rather than doubting it or thinking it shouldn't be happening.

The world is exactly as it should be

Edgar Mitchell was the sixth man to walk on the moon, and he regularly spoke to audiences about his time as an astronaut. One of the things he experienced while in space was a profound moment of awakening. In his book *Earthrise*, he writes about this awakening and how he began to see the stars and planets—the entire cosmos—as flawless and in sync. While on the moon, he looked to the left and saw infinity, perfection that extended into the beyond. Every single planet and every single star was perfectly aligned and in order, connected by an invisible thread of nothingness. He then looked to his right, and all he could see was this tiny blue planet, which was the size of a quarter from his vantage point. And he thought about how all humankind's troubles existed on that quarter—everything from traffic jams to war. Everything we think is important, all on that tiny blue quarter. In that moment, he felt enlightenment; he understood that everything in our lives was on purpose and on time, and that there was no such thing as coincidence. He felt that the world was exactly as it should be. [12]

Several key points can be extracted from Edgar Mitchell's experience on the moon. Firstly, we tend to worry about the tiny things in life, and at the end of the day, they don't mean a darn thing. Think about how insignificant all our stress would seem from the moon. But all too often we attach ourselves to these tiny matters. Secondly, an invisible intelligence allows this whole universe to hang together, from the tiniest cells within our body to the stars and the planets throughout the galaxies. I encourage you to reflect on this. It is not by mere chance or luck that we happen to be living on a piece of dust caught in a sunbeam; a piece of dust that's spinning at the right speed on the right axis in a perfect orbital pattern around the sun. There is a purpose to this planet, just as there is a purpose to your life.

To be Forever Young, see your world as an expression of the universe—as it is and not as you think it should be. Stop trying to control external

---

[12] Edgar Mitchell, Earthrise (Chicago Review Press, 2014), p. 43.

occurrences and rest in that peaceful awareness that everything is being handled for you. There are no mistakes or coincidences, and everyone and everything arrives exactly on time. This awareness will allow you to experience the world with a sense of purpose and direction. Instead of wondering why things are happening to you, you can instead accept these things as teachings disguised in life's quirky outfits. Consider author Jackson Kiddard's words, which wrap up this chapter beautifully.

"Anything that annoys you is for teaching you patience. Anyone who abandons you is for teaching you how to stand up on your own two feet. Anything that angers you is for teaching you forgiveness and compassion. Anything that has power over you is for teaching you how to take your power back. Anything you hate is for teaching you unconditional love. Anything you fear is for teaching you courage to overcome your fear. Anything you can't control is for teaching you how to let go and trust the universe."

See the world as purposeful and watch your worries, stresses, and problems melt away. See the world as a Forever Young.

Affirmation

Everything that shows up in my life has a purpose. I know that all my experiences are great lessons in disguise—lessons that are necessary for me to go through in order to grow into the person I was meant to be. Without troubles, nothing is learned; therefore, I welcome tribulations with open arms and take them lightly and lovingly. I am always in the right place at the right time and everything that shows up has its place and its purpose.

I am Forever Young

7

RULE YOUR THOUGHTS, RULE YOUR WORLD

"Whatever you hold in your mind will tend to occur in your life. If you continue to believe as you have always believed, you will continue to act as you have always acted. If you continue to act as you have always acted, you will continue to get what you have always gotten. If you want different results in your life or your world, all you have to do is change your mind."

-Unknown

Everything that you have ever attracted into your life started out as a thought—

intangible, formless, and noiseless in your head. Despite how immaterial thoughts may seem, they are in fact very real. And they are directly related to your mental, physical, and spiritual health. As mentioned earlier in this book, every thought holds a vibration, and every vibration can be sensed, felt, and experienced by not only you, but by those around you as well. We feel happy around those who hold happy thoughts, and we feel sad around those who hold sad thoughts. Thus, it's crucial that we be mindful of our own thoughts and surround ourselves with those who do the same. The quality of our thoughts creates our reality, and if we wish to live lives of happiness then we must choose to fill our heads with happy thoughts. Your perception of the world and how you feel is nothing more than what you carry in your head. The Forever Youngs understand this concept, and are therefore selective about the thoughts they allow space for. They root their minds in peace and love, for these are essential ingredients for happiness.

Unfortunately, a peaceful mind can be hard to come by. Our minds tend to race with stressful thoughts of our own choosing. Consequently, we become overwhelmed, anxious, and afraid. And society bombards us with stimuli that work their way into our thinking: beauty commercials, celebrity gossip, politics, Tinder, Instagram, etc. All of these things can make for a turbulent mind. And this constant stimulation from the outside world can make us vulnerable to what the world tells us. We stop thinking and feeling for ourselves and instead let the world think for us. A crowded mind is a mind in distress, and a mind in distress creates a world of turmoil. A quiet mind is a mind at peace, and a mind at peace creates a world of tranquility. Turn off the TV, turn off the radio, turn off the computer, put down that phone, and sit in silence. Reflect on what you want to fill your mind with, for the world will always be striving to plug it with useless and immaterial banter.

Reduce and replace

It's not enough to have a mind that is still and quiet—it must also be grounded in positivity. So many of us live with mindsets that are self-defeating and rooted in fear. We can only achieve balance in our world if we learn to correct our minds; we must reduce the number of self-defeating thoughts we think each day and replace them with empowering ones. "Reduce and replace" can be a mantra to help you remember this principle throughout your day. By quieting our minds and replacing hateful thoughts with loving ones, we can eradicate stress and illness from our lives. Again, every illness has a vibration, and every vibration stems from a thought; correct the thought and you correct the illness. It all starts with the conversations you have with yourself. The following are some examples of thoughts that need to be reduced:

- I'm not thin enough.
- I'm not rich enough.
- I'm not smart enough.
- I'm not enough.
- I don't deserve it.
- What if I don't make it?
- What if others find out?
- What if they don't like me?
- What if I fail?
- I don't want to fail.
- Who am I to succeed?
- I'm scared.

All these thoughts originate from one master thought: "I'm not good enough." Once we understand that we are worthwhile simply because we exist, all our self-defeating language will shift to a language of empowerment—the language of the Forever Youngs. Any time one of these self-defeating thoughts presents itself to you, immediately replace it with one of the following counter-affirmations:

- What I desire is already on its way.
- My past has no bearing on my current/future state of affairs.
- I regret nothing, for everything has been a lesson learned for me.
- I know I am always in the right place at the right time; there are no accidents in this perfect world.
- I live in a world that is nurturing and loving, and everything I see reflects that.
- I am worthy of receiving love and attention, and I will attract the right partner into my life.
- I approve of who I am, regardless of others' opinions.
- The abundance of the universe is for everyone and everything—all I need to do is tune in to it.
- Life is meant to be taken lightly.
- I am successful in every undertaking I pursue.

- I am more than good enough, and I deserve only the best.

Saying these affirmations to yourself every morning can have a significant positive impact on your entire day. If you make the mental effort every day to remind yourself you are worthy and special, transformation will occur in your life. You will experience happiness more often and more frequently. We must learn to train the uncontrolled mind to think in this way, as it has been conditioned to be critical. The ability to enjoy life starts with how we think. So start every day by filling your mind with loving and nurturing thoughts, the thoughts of the Forever Youngs.

The biology of stress

Consider how stress affects the physical body. Stress (which is a result of thoughts) increases cortisol levels in the bloodstream, and cortisol raises blood pressure. High blood pressure creates ulcers, weakens the immune system, and puts the body in a state of fear and anxiety (all very real and measurable biological responses). The connection between our thoughts and our physiology is material, so we must exercise great mindfulness to prevent our thoughts from running wild. It's no surprise that we see stress-related illnesses pop up everywhere in society. We create our own sicknesses simply by thinking stressful thoughts all day long. So many of us work hard on sculpting the perfect body through weight training and cardio but forget to work out the most powerful and influential muscle in the body—the brain. We need to shift our focus to this part of the body and work on the internal dialogue that drives so much of our realties. The quality of our world is determined by the quality of our thoughts. Think healthy thoughts and your body will respond accordingly.

Stress sells, negativity sells, gossip sells, drama sells. The business of negativity is a very lucrative one, which is why we see so much of it. We're drawn to dramatic reality TV, negative news, celebrity gossip, and conflict. It's no wonder everyone is stressed out. Many of the most profitable companies in the world sell the "you're not good enough" idea. According to the latest market research by Lucintel, the global beauty market is a trillion-dollar industry. [13] And we're mesmerized by it. Can you imagine how many companies would go bankrupt if everyone felt

---

[13] http://www.cosmeticsdesign.com/Market-Trends/Global-beauty-market-to-reach-265-billion-in-2017-due-to-an-increase-in-GDP

whole, complete, and worthwhile regardless of their appearance, values, and/or beliefs? The world is constantly telling us what we should look like, whom we should be like, and what we should act like, and this can make us feel inadequate. Stop paying attention to what the world has in mind for you. Instead, centre yourself by quieting your mind and choosing to think thoughts that strengthen you. Listen to your unique inner world and disregard the external world and all its drama, for peace will never be found in listening to something outside of yourself.

The power hour

At certain times throughout the day, we are more receptive to the power of affirmations. These times will be different for everyone. Only when the mind is at peace, when internal dialogue and mental chatter is at a minimum, can we be open to receiving messages. During these moments when the mind is still, not only are we able to receive guidance from higher energies, but also, our positive affirmations have a more profound and amplified effect. My mind is most at peace in the early mornings, so this is when I say my affirmations. Of course you can do so at any time, but again, they are most effective when we are clearheaded and undistracted. To find your "power hour," be mindful of the moments throughout the day when you are most relaxed.

Early in the morning, during my power hour, I reflect on what I enjoy about myself, what I'm grateful for, and what excites me in my life. During your power hour, it's important to not just say your affirmations for the sake of saying them—you must also feel the emotion behind the words you're expressing. It's the feeling that will change your thinking patterns, not the words. The words are meaningless and empty without energy and emotion behind them. With conviction, say to yourself:

"I am worthwhile. I need not chase after anything to be complete. My existence is profoundly valuable and miraculous. Today love will surround me and fill my mind. Today I choose to vibrate at a higher frequency. Life is safe and nurturing. Whatever I need in this life comes to me at exactly the right time. I trust the process of life to lead me to my higher good." This affirmation is somewhat general, but you get the idea. Tailor your words to create an affirmation that resonates with you and your desires.

If you're having trouble creating an affirmation that resonates with you, gently direct your attention to a time you felt good. Imagine a moment when you experienced love in your life. You'll find that the background noise will soon fade and you'll be filled with a feeling of contentment. If you have trouble contemplating what love feels like, I encourage you to reflect on the words of Emmet Fox, which is a powerful affirmation in and of itself:

"There is no difficulty that enough love will not conquer; no disease that enough love will not heal; no door that enough love will not open; no gulf that enough love will not bridge; no wall that enough love will not throw down; no sin that enough love will not redeem. It makes no difference how deeply seated may be the trouble; how hopeless the outlook; how muddled the tangle; how great the mistake. A sufficient realization of love will dissolve it all. If only you could love enough, you would be the happiest and most powerful being in the world."

Reflect on these words during your power hour, and you will carry the vibration of love within you, which will only attract more love.

Decluttering your mind

There was a time when my life was cluttered. I was constantly overbooking myself, spreading myself too thin, attempting to spend time with too many people all at once. I had too much to do and not enough time to recharge and reconnect with myself. My physical environment was cluttered as well. I had mountains of paper and receipts, piles of clothes that hadn't been worn in ages, and tons of miscellaneous items that served no purpose for me. However, as I became more self-aware I started to see that the culprit was my cluttered mind. Hundreds of self-defeating thoughts were racing through my mind each day. I was constantly worried about things that hadn't yet happened, and overanalyzed every situation. My mind was distraught, and as a result, my physical environment followed suit.

Your physical space is often a reflection of the inner workings of your mind. Thus, a cluttered house full of junk might represent a mind filled with low-energy thoughts. Many of us compensate for feeling not good enough by accumulating as much "stuff" as possible to fill that void. I'm not saying you should immediately throw out everything you own and clean your closet. Instead, simply adopt the Forever Young mindset and be more mindful of what you're holding on to in your home and in your life—are there things that serve no purpose? Consider that room you haven't cleaned in ages. What's holding you back from letting go of the things inside it? Or clearing it out completely?

When I started to work on stabilizing my thoughts, my mind learned how to become quiet and still. Consequently, my physical and social environments responded accordingly. I left behind friends who no longer resonated with me, I donated the clothes and shoes that I no longer wore, and I threw out the old receipts collecting dust in my filing cabinet. When we cleanse our minds, we habitually cleanse the physical space around us as well.

Resting your restless mind

Try this short exercise, which will help turn down the volume in your head. Close your eyes and be attentive to whatever is going on around you. Don't listen to any one sound over another. Just be casually observant. As you focus your attention on the sounds around you, you'll notice that your mind will start talking to you. But whatever it says, simply observe it with no attachment. Refocus your attention on the sounds outside your head without analyzing them. Just listen to them. Again, your mind will start a conversation with you. And again, refocus your attention on the sounds around you. This is the practice of being present. Keep doing this for about thirty minutes. You can also do this with your eyes open, anywhere, at any time of day—while walking in nature, playing catch with your dog, sipping a coffee, or doing a crossword. All of these are opportunities to quiet your mind, opportunities to be fully present in the moment without anticipating the future or reflecting on the past. It is not our natural state of being to have a mind in anarchy, bombarded with thoughts.

To reconnect with that essence within, we must learn to dive beneath the thousands of thoughts that blitz our consciousness, and shift our attention to the here and now. The Forever Youngs understand this and work at quieting their minds each day through some form of meditation. They understand that a mind at ease leads to a life of peace and harmony; a mind at ease is able to attract and create that which it desires. With an overactive mind, your ability to attract and create is restricted. As Sri Nisargadatta Maharaj said, "A quiet mind is all you need. All else will happen rightly, once your mind is quiet."

Quiet your mind by entrenching yourself in the present moment, by filling your head with thoughts of confidence rather than doubt, and by ridding yourself of all the unnecessary mental baggage that you've been carrying with you throughout the years.

Affirmation

My world responds to whatever thoughts I feed my mind. I control my life because I control my thoughts. I choose to fill my mind with empowering thoughts. I do this by quieting my world through meditation, replacing self-doubt with self-confidence, and grounding myself in the present moment. I experience the present moment more fully by letting go of my personal history and by embracing my future with joy and excitement. As I advance my consciousness to higher-vibrating energies, my physical world responds accordingly.

I am Forever Young

8

HAPPY FOOD, HAPPY YOU

What your food eats, you eat, and what your food feels, you feel.

Everything we eat has a profound effect on our health. What we ingest quite literally makes up our bodies in some way. For example, protein makes up our muscles, calcium makes up our bones, carbohydrates make up our energy, fats make up our hormones, minerals make up our regulators, and water makes the whole system run smoothly and effectively. The chemical components of the food we eat serve their own unique purpose in the body. If we want to create a life that feels good, we need to eat foods that nourish and sustain the physical body and all its biological processes. And we also need to eat foods that nourish and sustain the mind, emotions, and soul.

We've discussed how everything in the universe is energy. From the people we meet to the thoughts we think, everything carries a vibration that either empowers or disempowers us. The foods we consume are no different. The vibrations of the food we eat enter us directly and ultimately become part of our energetic field. Healthy foods have higher vibrations, which make us feel good, whereas unhealthy foods have lower vibrations, which make us feel bad. The better we eat, the higher the food vibration, the better we feel.

What your food eats, you eat

The Forever Youngs know that to experience high levels of happiness throughout our lives, we need to be mindful of the food we eat and the energy it holds. I'm not talking about the kind of energy that relates to calories—rather, I'm referring to the food's essence. Whether it's a mushroom, a fig, or a cow, all food builds up energy over the course of its life, right up to the moment it's plucked, picked, or cooked. Just like humans, food carries memories, feelings, and experiences, and all of these elements determine the health of the substance to be ingested. Radiant foods grow out of an environment that contains plenty of water, nutrients, and affection. Foods low in energy grow out of an environment of scarcity, malnourishment, and fear.

Let's look at an example: a cow raised in a hostile environment. On some ranches, once a cow is born it is immediately put on a regimented diet and confined to a small fenced area. Its diet will be composed mainly of corn, milo, barley, and oats—but not the natural versions of these grains. No, these grains will have been infused with dozens of chemicals and fillers manufactured by agrochemical organizations in order to promote the cow's growth. A bigger cow means more meat means more profit for the farmers and the agrochemical companies. Seems like a no-brainer, doesn't it? From a business perspective, yes, it's lucrative, but it comes at a great cost to not only the cow's health, but yours as well.

Bovine somatotropin is one of the many synthetically created hormones added to the cow's food supply, and an overwhelming amount of evidence-based research links high dosages of bovine somatotropin with infertility, cancer, infections, digestive disorders, and many other complications, too many to list. While the cow produces this hormone naturally, it does so in very small increments over its life span. However, when this hormone is administered in large doses, the cow grows much bigger than it normally would, and produces greater volumes of milk. Again, this is profitable for the farmers and the agrochemical companies but is in no way beneficial to the cow. The excess hormones running through its bloodstream create endless complications. Due to the chemical saturation, the cow's endocrine system is now completely out of balance, confused as to what hormones to produce and in what quantities. Consequently, the cow's body works overtime, and as a result, its immune system weakens and becomes vulnerable to attack. This ultimately creates stress, fatigue, pain, and illness for the cow. Its energy (physical, mental, and emotional) begins to deteriorate.

Now why on earth should we care, you ask? I mean, as long as you get a delicious burger on your plate, you're happy, right? Well, aside from the sad fact that the cow has a war going on within its body, at the end of the day, we consume everything this creature has ingested throughout its lifetime. What the cow eats, we eat. Traces of the artificially produced hormones, steroids, and fillers that once filled the cow can be found in the meats that we purchase from the grocery store. And if these synthetically produced chemicals cause cancer, impotency, infertility, and other disorders in the cow, then what makes you think it would be any different for humans? And that's not all. Not only do we consume the toxic substances, we also consume the animal's toxic experiences, emotions, and feelings.

What your food feels, you feel

What our food experiences is passed on to us at an energetic level. You might think this is an outrageous claim, but it's backed by basic science. Let's continue with the example of the cow. Though a cow's life might seem dull, in fact it's quite stressful if the animal is raised for the purpose of generating as much profit as possible. Livestock is often subject to fear, hostility, and poor living conditions, especially in the moments leading up to its slaughter. This experience can be quantified and measured on a biological level, as it alters the animal's physical makeup.

Cortisol (the stress hormone) is produced in the cow's endocrine system when the animal finds itself in a stressful situation. Cortisol is designed to give the animal energy to survive and tolerate high levels of pain. However, prolonged and sustained exposure to this hormone is incredibly damaging to the immune system and the animal's psychological state. This hormone builds up within the cow's tissues over its lifetime (if subject to stress) and spikes right before the animal is slaughtered and shipped away for consumption. As a result, traces of this cortisol will remain in the meat. Essentially, fear and stress (cortisol by-products) live within the fibres of this meat and are passed on to us when we sit down for that lovely steak dinner. Again, we not only consume the chemicals that resided in the cow's food, but also the emotions and feelings that the cow experienced, through hormonal residue.

The next time you're at a fast-food restaurant, check in with how you're feeling after you eat. Are you energized? Refreshed? Or do you feel tired? Sick to your stomach? Anxious or frustrated? On the other hand, eat fruits, vegetables, free-range chicken, or non-medicated beef and then check in with yourself. I bet you'll feel much more at peace than you felt after eating any sort of processed, artificially grown, or emotionally distraught foods. We are what we eat. And if we want to be Forever Young and experience higher levels of awareness and health, then we need to be mindful not only of our thoughts, but also of what we put inside our bodies.

Food is your medicine drawer

By combining loving thoughts with foods that are rich in nutrients, we can cure illness in the body. This combination is by far more powerful than any medicine at your local pharmacy. Approximately 60 million deaths each year are linked to obesity and anxiety! Imagine how many early deaths and stress-related illnesses could be prevented if we just learned to think loving thoughts and ingest high-vibrational foods. Imagine how much money the healthcare system would save if people just learned to lighten up a little bit and controlled what they put in their bodies. The billions upon billions of taxpayers' dollars saved could go towards educating the public on the root causes of illness rather than towards bandage solutions (surgery, liposuction, artery bypasses) that only suppress the issues.

In the West, the idea that food is medicinal and therapeutic has until recently been largely viewed with skepticism and doubt. Eastern cultures, however, have held this belief for thousands of years and have implemented it in their everyday lives. In Eastern cultures, food is considered to be more than just calories used in the production of energy; it's something with which we have a relationship—good energy in will flush bad energy out, and bad energy in will flush good energy out. They see food as healing, and instead of opting for that aspirin or surgical procedure, they look to the gifts Mother Nature has to offer. Here in North America, much of the population chooses food based on taste and convenience. The temptation that surrounds us is hard to resist. Just walk ten minutes in any direction and you'll probably come across a fast-food joint offering your taste buds delicious fulfillment—perhaps a salty, juicy beef patty nestled in a soft, chewy, warm bun. And you can wash it down with a cold, crisp soda. It screams: "Eat me, eat me." However, this meal, among many others we consume on a regular basis, lacks high-vibrating energy, and what lacks high-vibrating energy also lacks nutritional value. The beef patty is processed and filled with hormones and antibiotics (that cow we talked about), and the bun contains chemicals we can hardly pronounce; specifically, one called *azodicarbonamide*, which is linked to asthma and a list of other complications. That cold, crisp soda contains around twelve teaspoons of sugar (our maximum daily intake), and if an aluminum nail were to be left in such a liquid, it would dissolve completely in four days. What sort of effect does that liquefied sugar have on our stomach lining? We won't touch on those golden crispy fries for the time being—those are just way too good to pass up!

But seriously, we need to be asking ourselves these questions before we eat: "Where's the nutrition in this meal?" and "How will I feel after consuming this?" If your answers are "There's not many nutrients in here," and "I will likely feel sick," order something else—that meal is not promoting the well-being of your body but hindering it. Of course, it's fine to splurge and have cheat days occasionally. Just do so mindfully, and refrain from prolonged exposure to foods that bring your energy levels down.

Empowering meals

Let's look at a typical "Eastern" meal: black rice with mushrooms and a side of protein (usually a lean meat such as lamb or duck garnished with peppermint). The black rice is rich in antioxidants, which prevent inflammation and the oxidation of molecules, which is incredibly dangerous—the process is known to produce free radicals within the body. Free radicals are rogue cells that attack healthy cells, causing accelerated aging, cancer, fatigue, and a whole whack of other issues. These radicals appear when we consume poor-quality substances such as grease, alcohol, cigarettes, air pollutants, and pesticides. Thus, it's wise to consume foods that are rich in antioxidants as much as possible. Next, the mushrooms are loaded with copper, vitamin B5, selenium, vitamin B2, and many other vitamins and minerals that allow our bodies to function effectively. Copper increases energy and contributes to the strength of our connective tissues, and vitamin B5 is known to reduce stress and anxiety while boosting the immune system. Seems like a pretty good meal so far, doesn't it? Now for the lamb. Lamb meat is highly nutritious if the animal was raised in an environment conducive to its well-being and it ingested food that contained no synthetic hormones, steroids, and antibiotics. This meat is a home run, as it contains protein, niacin, and iron. Protein builds and repairs tissues in the body; niacin supports brain function and improves cholesterol levels if they're out of balance (niacin can also be used to treat migraines and solve circulatory issues in the endocrine system); and iron plays a significant role in the production of hemoglobin, which helps carry oxygenated blood (which every cell needs to survive) throughout the body. Lastly, the dash of peppermint is small but powerful, as it serves to ward off irritable bowel syndrome and abdominal pains. Every substance in this dish contributes to our well-being in some way. We can heal our bodies the natural way, through the food we eat rather than through human-made medications. Now, ask yourself those two questions again: "Where's the nutrition in this meal?" and "How will I feel after consuming this?" Your answers in this case would be "This is rich in nutrients," and "I will likely feel more energized and alert." You've chosen the healthy option.

Hydration

We are also what we drink. And the healthiest option for a nice, cold, refreshing drink? You guessed it—water. Or did you? Many of us don't drink enough water each day to maintain an optimal level of health in the body. Water is crucial in sustaining and balancing the body's functions. It flushes toxins from our systems, regulates our internal temperature, allows for proper digestion and nutrient absorption, and protects our tissues, organs, and joints.

Despite its wonderful benefits, water often falls way down on the list of desirable drinks, behind lower-vibrating fluids such as soda, energy drinks, alcohol, fruit juice, and tea. While some of these can be beneficial in moderation, any positive influence they have on our systems doesn't compare to water's. Our bodies are comprised mostly of water, so doesn't it make sense to replenish ourselves with what we're made of? Ask yourself, "How much water am I drinking throughout the day?" Is it four glasses? Seven? Eight? Or nowhere near these numbers? According to many health institutions around the globe, on average we need between eight to twelve cups of water per day to keep our cells hydrated and functioning correctly.

When we are dehydrated, we are energetically out of balance, and when we are out of balance, we become susceptible to illness.

Hydration and healing

Dr. Sebi was a world-renowned pathologist, herbalist, and naturalist who spent most of his life teaching the public about the connection between ingestion and health. He taught that all diseases originate from what we eat and drink, and that by eating and drinking better, we can eradicate illness in the body. (And while I agree with his theory, I would add one more element. The quality of our thoughts determines our health as well. If we can pair happy thoughts with healthy eating, THEN we can achieve perfect balance in the body.) Dr. Sebi's approach to healing was essentially based on the premise of ridding the body of stagnate toxins, such as mucus.

This is where the healing properties of water come in. The more water we consume, the more effective our body is at removing toxins. In scientific terms: when we are hydrated, every cell in the body functions better. More specifically, the kidneys, which are responsible for ridding wastes from the body, can filter out the toxins more easily. In spiritual terms: when we are hydrated, the body is better able to flush out slower vibrating energy. This "congestion of energy" clears up as we drink more water. Simply put, water purifies the body by removing blocked energy.

When we feel out of balance or sick, usually the first thing we do is consult a doctor. And rarely ever do we hear the doctor say, "Drink more water." Instead, we are prescribed a chemical that was manufactured in a lab somewhere. Luckily, while chemical prescriptions are still common in medical practices today, there is a shift occurring in the world of health. Doctors are becoming more open to and interested in alternative methods of healing. For example, a doctor in Turkey prescribes water and fasting as his primary treatment. His justification? It rejuvenates our cells by allowing the digestive system a much-needed break from foods and flushes out the residual toxins that reside within us. Many of his patients have claimed to have been healed from their ailments after participating in the fast-and-water treatment plan. [14] And this is not an isolated event. Other medical professionals advocate the same treatment plan. Dr. Fereydoon Batmanghelidj, who practices on the western side of the globe, can often be heard saying, "You're not sick, you're thirsty."

These medical professionals all follow the same principle: purify through hydration. In your own experience, have you ever noticed how good you feel after downing three or four glasses of water? Do you feel lighter and more energized? It may seem as if dysfunction disappears by magic. If you're experiencing a headache, drink water, for usually this is a sign of dehydrated cells in the brain; if you're experiencing arthritis, drink water, for this could be a sign of water shortage in the joint areas. Of course drinking water alone isn't the cure to all your problems, but it will surely aid in

---

[14] https://www.youtube.com/watch?v=B8gp5IrOnOY

clearing out the stagnate energies from your body, and will assist you on the road to perfect health.

Every food and liquid, just like every thought, has a vibration to it, and every vibration either raises our energetic field or weakens it. To be Forever Young, be mindful of the kind of energy you put in your body. Choose high-vibrational foods that enhance the quality of your life. Instead of feeling slow, lethargic, and sick after you eat, you can choose to feel vibrant, young, and clearheaded, for what you ingest becomes ingrained in every cell of your being. Every food has a unique and specific set of healing properties. We don't need to search for solutions in pills. If we can shift our mindset to that of love and our diet to one that is rich in nutrients, we can reinvent our bodies, enjoy good mental health, and reach that level of conscious awareness at which the Forever Youngs reside.

Affirmation

Everything I ingest carries a vibration. High-vibrational foods grow out of an environment of nutrition and love; low-vibrational foods grow out of an environment of scarcity and fear. I choose to ingest foods and liquids that are high in energy and thus allow me to feel energized, peaceful, and content. Through loving thoughts and a nutritious diet, I find myself in perfect health and happiness.

I am Forever Young

9

PUSH THROUGH FAILURE

There is no fear in the world, only people thinking fearful thoughts.

If there's something you want, do everything in your power to go out there and get it. Not chasing your dreams, your excitement, and your desires is the biggest disservice you can do to yourself. What holds people back from pursuing the things they want? Usually, it's simply this thought: "I'm afraid to fail." This thought permits people to stay stuck, confined, and in a routine. This is not a Forever Young thought.

Imagine what your life would look like if you had no regard for the fear of failure. You would be at peace with every outcome in your life! Whether you succeeded or not, you would be content with the result. Thus, when you let go of attachment to fear, you advance with confidence and often find exactly what you're looking for. The thought of failure isn't something that we humans take lightly. But you have been blessed with life, and this life is yours to shape and mould as you see fit. What is it that you want during your brief stint here? Whom do you want to be? How do you want to be remembered? As we've discussed, so many people live their lives doing what's best for the tribe and not what's best for them. They look for the answers on the outside, when really, they know the answers—the answers are within themselves. So many people wake up every morning to jobs they find "okay," to relationships they find "okay," only to find out in their mid-fifties on some idle Tuesday that their whole existence has just been "okay." These are the people who let the fear of failure, the fear of uncertainty, and the fear of change take precedence.

The Forever Youngs see a life without failure as a life that has been played safe, and a life that has been played safe is a life that wasn't really lived at all. They welcome failure with open arms, embrace it, feel it, and continue forward. This is what makes them great. This is what separates them from the masses.

The court versus the stands

In your life, are you playing on the court? Or are you sitting in the stands?

The Takers and the Floaters sit in the stands. They choose to drift through life and play it safe. They feel more comfortable following rather than leading. Conversely, the Forever Youngs take risks and take charge of their world. They have no desire to sit on the sidelines and watch others make something of themselves. They choose to participate in the game. The reason so many people stick to the stands is because it's a place they can hide from judgment and fear. Just as there are always more people in the stands than on the court, there are more people motivated by fear than risk in this world. The group mentality in the stands is "I'm afraid to fail, to look bad." The people in the stands can criticize and blame others without being challenged and put in the spotlight themselves—they aren't willing to take that sort of heat. Instead, they choose a life of mediocrity.

But your living life in the stands doesn't do much for the world. It doesn't take any effort, any motivation, any drive, any passion, any energy, or any risk to be average, to go unnoticed, to remain unscathed, unharmed, untouched. To live a life that is guarded and in line with society's expectations is safe, cozy, and predictable.

The next time you feel scared to try something, remember that no matter what you do and no matter where you go, no matter whom you meet or how hard you try, you will, without question, end up at the final destination we all share. Death is inescapable, no matter how safe you play it. And in those final breaths leading up to your last moments, while you reflect on your life, you will almost certainly wish you had swung for the fences, taken risks, and dared to be great.

Remember, we have absolutely nothing to lose, for we are born into this world with nothing and leave with nothing. When you fear failure, shift your mind to this thought: "So what? We all end up six feet underground anyway." Steve Jobs spoke about fear, failure, and death during his Stanford commencement speech in 2005: "Remembering that I'll be dead soon is the most important tool I've ever encountered to help me make the big choices in life. Almost everything—all external expectations, all pride, all fear of embarrassment or failure—these things just fall away in the face of death, leaving only what is truly important." 15

What are you putting off because you fear failure? What's the big worry? What's the worst that can happen, if you do fail? What's so scary, if we're all headed to the same resting ground anyway? Why not take those chances?

If you really want to seize this life, you must adopt the Forever Young mindset. Go outside your comfort zone, be content with setbacks, bend the rules, and say yes to life by giving it everything. The Forever Youngs embrace fear and embrace failure—and then they tell it to sit on the sidelines. Although they may feel fear, they don't let it immobilize them. They don't let it dictate the story of their life. Like Susan Jeffers says, "Feel the fear and do it anyway." Pursue what you want in this life, for trying and failing is far better than never trying at all.

---

[15] https://www.forbes.com/sites/moiraforbes/2011/10/05/steve-jobs-death-is-very-likely-the-single-best-invention-of-life/#5916468c29b0.

Affirmation

I have but one life, and I choose to live it on my terms. I will not fear failure, for this fear serves no purpose in my life. I am comfortable with taking risks, taking chances, and pursuing my goals. I take great comfort in this pursuit, for we all arrive at death's doorstep sooner or later. And when this hour comes, there will be nothing but joy in my heart, for I have dared to live the life I have imagined for myself.

I am Forever Young

FINAL THOUGHTS

We have within us a phenomenal power: the power to manifest our desires. There is a part of each of us that yearns for a deeper and richer experience of life, and it's time we listen to this inner knowing. Far too many people roam this world as Takers and Floaters. Far too many people are here physically but have checked out mentally, spiritually, and emotionally. Far too many people have lost their passion, their purpose, and simply wander through their remaining years going through the motions.

This doesn't have to be the case. Instead, we can be Forever Youngs. We can choose to rise above and let go of all the noise and negativity in the world. We can choose to align our thoughts with our purpose, passion, and desires. We can choose to move past the tribe, and not let society have any bearing on our inner world.

It is my hope that you rediscover that eternal youth within you—that you remain playful and childlike well into old age, for fun should always exist in your life. It is my hope that you let go of the fear surrounding your dreams and find the courage and peace to follow your intuition, for life is too short and too precious to be ordinary and bland. It is my hope that when drama unfolds in your world, you recognize it as purposeful and intentional, for everything and everyone is a teacher, guiding you to higher levels of awareness. What you're experiencing right now is exactly what you need to be experiencing. You are always in the right place, at the right time, and there is a purpose to everything. It is my hope that you leave the tribe behind and follow your inner calling. Only you know your truth and what others say or do has nothing to do with your divine mission. How people treat you reflects their reality, not yours. Cultivate your own garden, without worry or concern for your neighbours—everyone is on their own unique journey. It is my hope that you rid your mind of self-defeating thoughts and instead take moments throughout your day to nourish and feed your soul with loving and positive affirmations. It is my hope that you surround yourself with loving people, for those we associate with tend to determine our state of being. Find the visionaries, the risk takers, the deep talkers—the ones who have a sense of purpose—for you will rise up with them. It is my hope that you pamper your body with nourishing substances that empower you, for we are energetic beings taking on the energies in our foods and liquids.

It is my hope that one day you find everything you are looking for and grow into the kind of person who gives energy to this world and helps others in need. And above all, it is my hope that you remain Forever Young, in body, mind, and spirit.

THE AFFIRMATIONS

THE THREE KINDS OF PEOPLE

I choose to surround myself with people who bring out the best in me, not people who bring out the stress in me. I will work on correcting my thoughts so that I may experience a higher level of awareness in my life. This higher level of awareness will allow me to create and lead the life I have envisioned for myself.

I am Forever Young

LEAVE THE TRIBE BEHIND

I know that in this life, there will always be a critic, no matter what I decide to do or express. I choose to live my life based on my inner reality, and I disregard the beliefs and opinions of others. What other people think of me is a reflection of their reality and where they are in their karmic paths. Life is but a moment in eternity, and I will not concern myself with external beliefs, opinions, and ideas, for this is my unique journey.

I am Forever Young

BE PLAYFUL

I choose to live this life lightly, for I reside in a universe that is playful and recreational. I know my thoughts create my reality. Thus, I choose thoughts that help me to remain healthy and strong. I know that the cells in my body are a direct reflection of how I perceive the world. Therefore, I see myself as growing younger every day. Each day, my cells are replenished, repaired, and replaced. Each day they are in a healthier and more vital state. I am ageless, timeless, and full of positive thoughts.

I am Forever Young

YOU ARE NOT YOUR BODY

I know that I am an energetic being encapsulating a body, and that what constitutes my existence is beyond my physical form. I am what I choose to think about all day long, so I choose to think healthy thoughts that create good vibes within me. My cells are constantly being replaced and replenished, so the past has no bearing on my current state of affairs. From this moment forward I choose to experience high-vibrating energies that contribute to a life of perfect health.

I am Forever Young

QUIT WORRYING

I choose to walk this earth lightly with a carefree spirit, for worrying serves no purpose to my well being. It is my birthright to be joyous and happy, so I work at filling my mind with thoughts that allow me to feel this way. I choose to spend my time cultivating my own garden without concern for the tribe's ideas and opinions. This is my unique path that I have chosen, so I live it according to my terms and conditions.

I am Forever Young

TRUST THE TIMING OF YOUR LIFE

Everything that shows up in my life has a purpose. I know that all my experiences are great lessons in disguise—lessons that are necessary for me to go through in order to grow into the person I was meant to be. Without troubles, nothing is learned; therefore, I welcome tribulations with open arms and take them lightly and lovingly. I am always in the right place at the right time and everything that shows up has its place and its purpose.

I am Forever Young

RULE YOUR THOUGHTS, RULE YOUR WORLD

My world responds to whatever thoughts I feed my mind. I control my life because I control my thoughts. I choose to fill my mind with empowering thoughts. I do this by quieting my world through meditation, replacing self-doubt with self-confidence, and grounding myself in the present moment. I experience the present moment more fully by letting go of my personal history and by embracing my future with joy and excitement. As I advance my consciousness to higher-vibrating energies, my physical world responds accordingly.

I am Forever Young

HAPPY FOOD, HAPPY YOU

Everything I ingest carries a vibration. High-vibrational foods grow out of an environment of nutrition and love; low-vibrational foods grow out of an environment of scarcity and fear. I choose to ingest foods and liquids that are high in energy and thus allow me to feel energized, peaceful, and content. Through loving thoughts and a nutritious diet, I find myself in perfect health and happiness.

I am Forever Young

PUSH THROUGH FAILURE

I have but one life, and I choose to live it on my terms. I will not fear failure, for this fear serves no purpose in my life. I am comfortable with taking risks, taking chances, and pursuing my goals. I take great comfort in this pursuit, for we all arrive at death's doorstep sooner or later. And when this hour comes, there will be nothing but joy in my heart, for I have dared to live the life I have imagined for myself.

I am Forever Young

WRITE YOUR OWN AFFIRMATIONS

Manufactured by Amazon.ca
Bolton, ON